W9-BFS-076

Media, Markets, and Morals

Edward H. Spence is Senior Research Fellow at the Australian Research Council funded Special Research Centre for Applied Philosophy and Public Ethics (CAPPE), Australia, and Research Fellow at the 3TU Centre for Ethics and Technology, The Hague, Netherlands. He also teaches media ethics in the School of Communication and Creative Industries at Charles Sturt University, NSW, Australia. He is the author of *Advertising Ethics*, with Brett Van Heekeren (2005), *Corruption and Anti-Corruption: A Philosophical Approach*, with Seumas Miller and Peter Roberts (2005), *Ethics Within Reason: A Neo-Gewirthian Approach* (2006), and co-editor of *The Good Life in a Technological Age* (forthcoming), with Philip Brey and Adam Briggle.

Andrew Alexandra is Senior Research Fellow and Director of the Australian Research Council funded Special Research Centre for Applied Philosophy and Public Ethics (CAPPE) at the University of Melbourne. He has published *Police Ethics*, co-authored with J. Blackler and S. Miller (1997, 2006), *Private Military Companies: Ethics, Theory and Practice*, co-edited with D. Baker and M. Caparini (2008), and *Integrity Systems for Occupations*, co-authored with Seumas Miller (2010).

Aaron Quinn is Assistant Professor of Journalism at California State University, Chico. He has published work in academic journals, including *The Journal of Mass Media Ethics* and *The International Journal of Applied Philosophy*, and has contributed chapters to titles published by Oxford University Press and Broadview Press. He previously worked as a newspaper and magazine reporter, photographer, and editor.

Anne Dunn is Associate Professor in the Department of Media and Communications and Pro Dean Academic in the Faculty of Arts and Social Sciences at the University of Sydney. She has written on media ethics for academic journals, including *Ethical Space*, and is co-author with H. Fulton, R. Huisman, and J. Murphet of *Narrative and Media* (Cambridge University Press 2005). She spent more than 20 years working as a presenter, media researcher, journalist, producer, and director for commercial television, SBS, and for the ABC. Her work includes award-winning television and film documentaries.

Media, Markets, and Morals

Edward H. Spence,
Andrew Alexandra,
Aaron Quinn, and Anne Dunn

WILEY-BLACKWELL

A John Wiley & Sons, Ltd., Publication

This edition first published 2011
© 2011 Edward H. Spence, Andrew Alexandra, Aaron Quinn, and Anne Dunn

Blackwell Publishing was acquired by John Wiley & Sons in February 2007.
Blackwell's publishing program has been merged with Wiley's global Scientific,
Technical, and Medical business to form Wiley-Blackwell.

Registered Office
John Wiley & Sons Ltd, The Atrium, Southern Gate, Chichester, West Sussex,
PO19 8SQ, United Kingdom

Editorial Offices
350 Main Street, Malden, MA 02148-5020, USA
9600 Garsington Road, Oxford, OX4 2DQ, UK
The Atrium, Southern Gate, Chichester, West Sussex, PO19 8SQ, UK

For details of our global editorial offices, for customer services, and for information
about how to apply for permission to reuse the copyright material in this book
please see our website at www.wiley.com/wiley-blackwell.

The right of Edward H. Spence, Andrew Alexandra, Aaron Quinn, and Anne Dunn
to be identified as the authors of this work has been asserted in accordance with the
UK Copyright, Designs and Patents Act 1988.

Library of Congress Cataloging-in-Publication Data

Media, markets, and morals / Edward H. Spence, ... [et al.].
    p. cm.
Includes bibliographical references and index.
ISBN 978-1-4051-7547-0 (hbk : alk. paper) – ISBN 978-1-4051-7546-3 (pbk : alk. paper)
1. Mass Media–Moral and ethical aspects. 2. Mass media–Economic aspects. I. Spence, Edward H.
P94.M3618 2011
302.23–dc22

                                                                                    2010049300

A catalogue record for this book is available from the British Library.

This book is published in the following electronic formats: ePDFs ISBN 9781444396027;
ePub ISBN 9781444396034

Set in 10.5/13.5pt, Palatino by Thomson Digital, India

1   2011

Contents

Acknowledgments

I wish to thank the following people and institutions for their contribution to the completion of this book: Professor Philip Brey and the VICI research team at the Philosophy Department at the University of Twente, the Netherlands, where part of this book was completed during my three-year research fellowship at that institution; The Centre for Applied Philosophy and Public Ethics (CAPPE), Charles Sturt University, for their support; my co-authors Aaron Quinn, Andrew Alexandra, and Anne Dunn for their faith, diligence, and patience; Kaye Spence for her love and support throughout this project; and last but not least on behalf of my co-authors and myself I would like to express our deep thanks and gratitude to the editorial team of Wiley-Blackwell, Jeff Dean, Michael Boylan, Tiffany Mok, Jacqueline Harvey, and Helen Gray for all their support and encouragement and also to Claire Dunn for her invaluable assistance in helping with the editing of the draft chapters of this book.

Edward H. Spence

My thanks to my family, Peter, Alice, James, and Claire, for their always positive and supportive attitude and for gently keeping me (more or less) to deadline. I add special thanks to Claire Dunn for her perceptive editorial comments on the draft chapters, and to the Faculty of Arts at the University of Sydney for invaluable research assistance.

Anne Dunn

Acknowledgments

I'd like to thank the many colleagues who helped shape these ideas, most prominently the co-authors of this manuscript. I'd also like to thank my very large extended family for its long-lasting support through years of academic pursuit. Most of all, I'd like to thank my father and sister, whose guidance and love have been central to a life well lived.

Aaron Quinn

1

Introduction

Aims and Objectives

We live, as we are often told, in the Information Age. That age has been made possible by technological advances. Over the past hundred years or so the development of recording devices such as cameras and audio and video recorders have allowed us to capture, store, and reproduce images, text, and sound much more easily than in the past. More recently, enormous strides in electronic technology have produced devices such as radio, television, and computers, which can process vast amounts of data and transmit them accurately and cheaply across large distances to huge audiences around the world. Smart phones such as the iPhone can do all this and much more at the touch of an icon on a screen. This kind of information and communication technology (ICT) puts the world at our fingertips.

Media, Markets, and Morals, First Edition. Edward H. Spence, Andrew Alexandra, Aaron Quinn, and Anne Dunn.
© 2011 Edward H. Spence, Andrew Alexandra, Aaron Quinn, and Anne Dunn. Published 2011 by Blackwell Publishing Ltd.

Important as these technological developments are, they have been only one of the elements that have produced the Information Age. The other major element has been the growth of organizations – "the media" – dedicated to the provision of information to the public through the channels of mass communication opened up by those developments. The media,[1] so understood, has become part of the fabric of our everyday life. We are likely to decide what clothes we put on in the morning on the basis of the weather report we have read in the newspaper, or seen on TV. We will divert ourselves as we commute to work or school by listening to music on the radio or our iPod: when we reach our destination we might discuss information which we have gathered from the media about the state of the nation, the latest Hollywood film or scandal, or the latest baseball, cricket, or football results, or retail the views of our favorite media pundit. In times of war or natural disaster we cluster around televisions or click onto media websites to keep up with the latest news. Huge amounts of money are spent on advertising globally in an attempt to influence the food we eat, the clothes we wear, the cars we drive, the holidays we take, what we drink. Even the way we vote for candidates for political office is influenced by their ability to present themselves in an appealing way on television and radio.

Given its size and importance, the media can be placed alongside politics, education, the military, culture, and religion as one of the fundamental institutions to shape (and to be shaped by) contemporary society. Each of these institutions has its own distinctive ethical demands, challenges, and temptations: the so-called *role morality* which applies to them and the people who play a part in them.

A theoretical account of a given role morality rests on two bases. First, an identification of the particular function(s) or role(s), which an institution is supposed to play in the life of a society: the military is supposed to protect us from external usurpation, the police to uphold law and order, the education system to give us the skills we need to become autonomous, socially and economically competent citizens, and so on. Second, an account of the current conditions within which the institution must function. A practicable institutional role morality will specify how the institution's function can be realized in the context of those conditions. Such a morality, then, is sensitive to the realities of its social setting, and as those realities change so must it. Think, for example, how what counts as an adequate education has changed over the past century, as the world has become more complex and the relations between the sexes have altered. An education system which would have served its purpose a hundred years ago when most people could function perfectly well with a primary school education would now clearly be seen as highly inadequate.

This is a book about the role morality of the media, both "old" and "new." Our first aim is to develop an overarching account of that morality. To do so, we begin by looking to the primary function of the media. As we see it, that function is to provide information to its audience. We then turn to a consideration of the main factors currently shaping and constraining the way in which that function is and can be realized. These include information and communication technologies but also, importantly, the domination of the media by large organizations, many of which are multimillion-dollar, powerful commercial enterprises. In the light of those considerations we can then address our second aim: to apply our account of the role morality of the media to particular issues which arise in media ethics, including both specific morally problematic practices and the question of how to promote ethical behavior within the media.

The extent to which we have succeeded in achieving our aims can be measured against two yardsticks. The first of these is how well our approach fits with and grounds clear moral intuitions about good and bad behavior. Let us consider two cases where members of the media have acted in ways which clearly exemplify, respectively, good and bad behavior.

Ed Murrow and "A Report on Senator Joseph McCarthy"

In the early 1950s Joseph McCarthy, Senator from the US state of Wisconsin, launched an anti-communist crusade, exploiting the fearful atmosphere of the Cold War to summon up the specter of a country riddled with internal enemies in positions of influence. Without scruple, McCarthy implied that government agencies, as well as the media and entertainment industries, were havens for subversion. In a 1950 speech he asserted that

> The reason why we find ourselves in a position of impotency is not because the enemy has sent men to invade our shores, but rather because of the traitorous actions of those who have had all the benefits that the wealthiest nation on earth has had to offer – the finest homes, the finest college educations, and the finest jobs in Government we can give.

As chairman of the Senate Permanent Subcommittee on Investigations, McCarthy would subpoena witnesses on short notice – if they invoked the Fifth Amendment of the US Constitution, which protects against self-incrimination, McCarthy would call them "Fifth Amendment communists" and if he thought he could intimidate them, make them appear in public to be cross-examined by him. So pervasive was the Senator's influence on American society that the period in which he wielded power came to be known as "the McCarthy era."

While McCarthy's influence grew, so did that of a new form of mass media – television. In 1950, around 3 million Americans owned television sets: ten years later 50 million did. Advertisers quickly recognized the reach of television into America homes. By 1954 CBS-TV had become the biggest single advertising medium in the world. The relationship between the television networks and political power, on the other hand, was inevitably uneasy. Coupled with the visceral impact and immediacy of the medium, the ability of the networks to reach a vast audience threatened politicians' control of political discourse in a way that had not been true of older forms of media such as newspapers. At the same time, there were powerful forces encouraging the networks to support the status quo – they depended on the government for access to the publicly owned airwaves, and on their corporate sponsors for continuing profitability. Television and film workers who were accused of being communists, or who refused to answer McCarthy's questions, were "blacklisted" and denied work in the industry.

This is the background against which the actions of Edward R. Murrow, and his part in bringing about the end of McCarthyism, should be understood. In the early 1950s Murrow, already a popular radio journalist with a reputation for honesty and integrity, made the transition to the medium of TV. Together with his producer Fred Friendly, he developed the current affairs program *See it Now* (based on his successful radio show *Hear It Now*) on CBS. On March 9, 1954 Murrow broadcast a special edition of *See It Now* called "A Report on Senator Joseph McCarthy," which is seen as having been instrumental in the backlash against McCarthy and which would end his reign of terror. Given McCarthy's power and ruthlessness any attempt to publicly call him to account required a good deal of courage. Moreover, Murrow himself had been warned only a few months earlier that McCarthy had evidence of his having been "on the Soviet payroll." There was an added, implicit threat to the career of Murrow's brother, who was a general in the US Air Force. Murrow and his team had been preparing for the McCarthy report for over a year. CBS did not permit Murrow and Friendly to use CBS money to advertise the program, nor to use the network logo in the ads, so the journalist and his producer paid for newspaper advertisements themselves. But even though the chairman of CBS, Bill Paley, was close to the Republican Party and knew that Murrow's show would create a political firestorm, he made no attempt to interfere with it and just before it went to air he called Murrow to say, "Ed, I'm with you today, and I'll be with you tomorrow."

Much of "A Report on Senator Joseph McCarthy" consisted of McCarthy's own words, demonstrating his inconsistency, dishonesty, and thuggery. Calling on the American tradition of toleration and respect for civil liberties, Murrow concluded that

> We will not walk in fear, one of another, we will not be driven by fear into an age of unreason. If we dig deep, deep in our history and our doctrine and remember that we are not descended from fearful men, not from men who feared to write, to speak, to associate with, and to defend causes which were for the moment unpopular ...

After the broadcast, tens of thousands of letters, telegrams, and phonecalls poured into CBS, running 15 to 1 in Murrow's favor. In

December of that year, the US Senate voted to censure Joseph McCarthy, making him one of the few senators ever to be so disciplined; he died in hospital three years later.

"A Report on Senator Joseph McCarthy" is often referred to as "TV's finest hour."

Jayson Blair

On April 29, 2003 Howard Kurtz wrote a story in the *Washington Post* titled "N.Y. Times Article Bears Similarities to Texas Paper's." So striking was the overlap between a story written by *San Antonio Express-News* reporter Macarena Hernandez about a local woman whose son was missing in Iraq and that appearing a week later in the *New York Times* under the byline of Jayson Blair, that the editor of the *San Antonio Express-News* sent the editor of the *Times* a letter of complaint.

Within two weeks Blair, who had been a reporter on the *Times* for four years had resigned, as the story emerged of an astonishing pattern of fraud in the published work of a successful young journalist at the largest and most prestigious metropolitan newspaper in the United States. In its own report on the scandal the *Times* noted "problems" in many of Blair's articles, including almost half of those he had written after being promoted to cover national assignments, and detailed his modus operandi, including plagiarism, fabrication of comments, and selection of details from photographs to create the false impression that he had traveled to a scene he was supposedly reporting on, or talked to someone he was supposedly interviewing. What the *Times* found more difficult to explain was its own role: members of its staff had expressed misgivings about Blair throughout his time there, with its metropolitan editor in 2002 warning administrators in an email that "We have to stop Jayson from writing for the *Times*. Right now."

As the *Times* lamented, these events "represented a low point in the 152 year history of the newspaper." (New York Times 2003)

Murrow's actions are generally seen as heroic, while everyone thinks Blair's behavior is shameful. Up to a point we can explain our reactions through the use of our ordinary moral categories: Murrow acted bravely and stood up for free speech against the forces of repression; Blair was deceitful. But we need to be able to say more than this. Murrow acted well not just as a person but as a broadcaster. Moreover, he did not act alone; he relied on support and resources from his producer and sponsors. We noted that his broadcast is often referred to as "TV's finest hour." Similarly, concerns about Blair's ongoing fraudulent behavior should focus not simply on the harm he did to readers and colleagues but what it showed about the pressures under which even the most eminent, powerful, and well-resourced media organizations operate, and how those pressures are leading to outcomes that undermine the trust which is necessary for the successful functioning of the media. Implicit in these responses to these two cases is the idea that the media has special moral responsibilities. What are these responsibilities, where did they come from and who are accountable for them? The approach we adopt throughout this book is designed to answer questions such as these.

The second yardstick against which to measure our account of media role morality is the extent to which it helps to illuminate morally contentious issues in the media. For example, there is an ongoing debate about perceived trends towards greater media concentration and conglomeration (we consider this debate in more detail in Chapter 6). At the heart of many of the concerns expressed about those trends is the feeling that they are tending to subvert the proper functioning of the media, which is to inform its audiences truthfully, credibly, reliably, and in a trustworthy manner. But unless we have a well-worked account of what that function is, and the conditions under which it can be achieved, and furthermore, the conditions under which the media's function can itself be overridden by the higher moral claims of a universal public morality that applies equally to all of us by virtue of our common humanity, we cannot judge whether those concerns are well founded. The case studies we use throughout the book – real-life examples of morally interesting situations – serve as both tests and illustrations of our approach.

In the rest of this chapter we outline the contents of the book.

The Structure of the Book

Chapters 2, 3, 4: Surveying the ethical landscape

In the first part of this book we consider in broad terms the nature of media ethics. We have identified the provision of information as the essential function of the media. The very concept of information implies certain ethical responsibilities on the part of those who produce and disseminate it. Let us give a very simple example to help explain why. A student on her first day of university asks a member of staff how to find a building where her class is to be held. The staff member provides clear and accurate directions – he gives her the information she needs – and the student makes her way to class without difficulty. We can derive a number of general conclusions about the nature of information from this story. First, information involves both a sender and receiver. Second, it must be accurate – if the staff member had given the student the wrong location of the building she would have received either misinformation (the accidental or negligent provision of inaccurate information) or disinformation (the deliberate and purposeful provision of inaccurate information). Third, information must be accessible to its target audience – if the staff member had spoken in a language which the student could not understand, no information would have been provided. Finally, the receiver of the information must trust the sender: the student came to hold a new true belief (in other words, knowledge) because she took the fact that the staff member said that the building was in a particular location as a good reason to believe that it was. If she thought that the staff member lacked the relevant knowledge, or had no interest in accurately relaying the knowledge he did possess, she may not have accepted his testimony, even if it was in fact true.

Like the university staff member in the story, members of the media present themselves to the public as providers of information. Thus, the media takes upon itself certain behavioral obligations which are derived from the inherent nature of information itself. We define those collectively in Chapter 2, as the *inherent normative structure of information* (note that the word "normative" as used here simply refers to the norms, rules, or principles which determine and obligate the ways in which all disseminators of information, including the media, should behave). If, as we claim, the media's defining task is to provide information, it follows that its practitioners must adhere to a number of ethical obligations. First, they must try to ensure that what they present to others as information is accurate. Second, they must present information in a form that is accessible to target audiences. Finally, they need collectively to build and retain the trust of their audience, by ensuring, among other things, that the material they present is factual, credible, and reliable and that neither individually nor as organizations are they seen to have ulterior motives that might lead to the distortion or suppression of inconvenient truths. In Chapter 2 we also point out that role moralities must be consistent with, and constrained by, the morality that applies to us all simply by virtue of our common humanity, what we call *universal public morality*.

We noted above that an account of the role morality of an institution cannot simply be read off the function(s) it is supposed to serve, but must take into account salient facts about the setting within which the institution operates. A notable, indeed defining, fact about the media in modern societies is the centrality of (often very large) organizations involved in the media as businesses. Like any commercial enterprise, such organizations aim to stay profitable and return dividends to owners and shareholders and to maintain jobs for their employees. On the face of it, these are legitimate aims. However, conveying information accurately and fairly may not always be the best way to gain financial rewards: there is a tension between the information-related and money-making functions of commercial media organizations. Any attempt to understand the ethics of the media in societies such as ours must address this tension and the issues which arise from it. This is what we do in Chapter 3, where we argue that the money-making functions of the media should be seen not as ends in themselves, but rather as means to the ultimate end of the media, that is, to inform accurately, truthfully, credibly, reliably, and fairly. So understood, the various apparent ethical conflicts between the different functions disappear.

The media as we know it has been shaped by the technologies available for producing, gathering, and disseminating information. Given the expense and organizational complexity involved in reaching large audiences, individual disseminators of information have had to rely on, and be supported by, large media organizations. This has resulted in the growth of the media professions, such as journalism, photography, editing, and so on, whose members have developed specialized skills, which they sell to media organizations. These groups tend to foster a strong sense of collective identity in their members, transcending their relationship with any particular media organization. Part of that collective identity is a shared understanding of the role morality which applies to the group, in their role of providing information on matters of public interest or of interest to the public. In Chapter 2 we look at this role morality, focusing in the first instance on journalism. Particular roles require distinctive virtues. Technical skill is often a necessary component of such role-relative virtues. But it is not sufficient: a grasp of the way in which that skill should be used to further the defining purpose of the activity is also required. Professional media groups engage in an ongoing process of dialogue and negotiation to produce a working consensus as to what counts as morally acceptable practice, as we illustrate through a consideration of some recent well-known cases.

The specialized media professions arose because the technology they used to reach the public was costly and required a high level of expertise to operate. Correlatively, recent developments of cheaper and easier means of producing, recording, and transmitting information are allowing a far broader range of people to play the roles that have traditionally tended to be occupied by media professionals. This ever growing trend is breaking down the rigid distinction between producers and audiences. The growth of new, digital media, which we consider in Chapters 2 and 4, is a morally complex and challenging phenomenon. On the one hand, it broadens and "democratizes" the sources of information. On the other, it means that many of those who are now able to contribute to the media do not have the competence, or commitment to or interest in the professional role morality that has traditionally provided at least some guidance to media practitioners. In the new media what passes as information is often no more than mere opinion or opinionated, uninformed comment. And opinion, unlike information, need not be and often is not accurate, credible, reliable, or trustworthy. Information respects facts; opinions often do not.

Chapters 5, 6, 7: Navigating the ethical minefield

In the first part of the book, we developed an account of media role morality. In this section, we use that account to address some of the major systemic difficulties facing contemporary media organizations and workers.

One such issue is the delineation between different media fields, in particular journalism, advertising, and public relations. The skills which media professionals develop can often be applied across these fields. Many former journalists find work in public relations or advertising, for example. Moreover there is a complex interdependence between these fields. Newspapers and TV stations depend on advertising revenue to remain viable. Public relations (PR) people see the news media as an important avenue for presenting their clients in a favorable light to the public. In Chapter 5 we look at the relationship between journalism on the one hand and public relations and advertising on the other. Each of these activities has its particular primary purpose: journalism to inform, advertising to persuade, and public relations to present a client or a project in a favorable light. Each of these activities is legitimate within its own sphere. Problems arise, however, when what is actually an advertising message in the form of an *advertorial*, or a public relations advocacy in the form of a *media release,* are disguised to look like journalism commentary or news, in newspapers or on radio, television, and increasingly the Internet in so-called "independent" blogs. For those involved there are often powerful reasons for allowing this to happen: advertisers or PR people can exploit the credibility which journalism has with its audience to sell their persuasion messages more effectively, while journalists can benefit from receiving ready-made material. For the media this might seem like a win-win situation, but for the public such practices are a total loss. Such behavior is deceptive: it amounts at best to misinformation (the accidental or negligent dissemination of false "information") and at worst to disinformation (the deliberate and purposeful dissemination of false "information"). Moreover, its discovery subverts the very trust which is a condition for its success and which, as we have argued above, media organizations and their employees have an obligation to maintain simply by virtue of their role as information providers.

Even more crucially, actions which blur the distinction between journalism on the one hand, and advertising and public relations on the other, are a form of *corruption.* Such actions are not just bad in themselves; they also tend to undermine the very goals to which the media as an institution is supposed to be dedicated to achieving. Since the media itself is one of the primary bulwarks against corruption through its capacity to uncover and publicize wrongdoing, media corruption is particularly pernicious. Given human frailty it is impossible to stamp out corruption altogether. However, if we are clear about what counts as media corruption and can identify its major causal factors we are at least in a position to guard against and to respond to it. In Chapter 6 we consider the concept of corruption as it applies to the media. The notion of corruption as it applies to an institution, we claim, presupposes the prior notion of a morally legitimate institution, or a morally sound role. Media corruption involves actions or processes that tend to undermine individuals, organizations, or the media as a whole in carrying out their proper functions. In a word, it undermines their role morality. We draw on the account of the purposes of the media developed in the first part of the book to identify cases of corrupt practices, and to diagnose what makes them corrupt.

In Chapter 7 we deploy the account of media corruption developed in the previous chapter to illuminate ethical issues in photojournalism, particularly in relation to the manipulation of images. The old sayings "A picture is worth a thousand words" and "Seeing is believing" reflect both the density of information which can be transmitted pictorially, and the greater credibility of a photograph, compared to words. A photograph seems to have an inbuilt guarantee of truthfulness which words lack. No doubt this guarantee has always been somewhat shaky, but it has become especially dubious in the light of technical developments which have made the manipulation of photographic images, both in the camera and post-shoot, far easier than in the past. At the same time, such images have become ever more common as bearers of information. Photographs as they appear to viewers are the product of a series of choices made by a photographer, an editor, and so on. A central question we address in the chapter is which choices are consistent with the demands of media ethics, and which tend to deceive and lead to loss of trust between media and audience.

Chapters 8, 9: A sustainable ethical environment

An institutional role morality can be seen as having two interacting parts. The first is the content of that morality: the overall purposes of the institution, the means that can legitimately be used to achieve those purposes and the rights and duties of members of the institution. The second part specifies the institutional arrangements that should be put in place to ensure that the role morality is actually effective: how it is applied, promoted, and reinforced.

In Chapter 8 we look at means for the regulation of media ethics, and show how problematic such regulation is. In many areas of business, required standards of behavior are specified by the law. In traditional professions such as law and medicine, regulatory power is concentrated in the hands of professional bodies which set conditions, including ethical behavior, for qualifying and continuing to practice, and impose sanctions when those conditions are not met. However, both of these tools are unsuitable for the media since they are incompatible with the notion that is at the heart of an effective media, that of freedom of the press. Further, the structure of the media industry, with its dominance by large corporations, also generates problems for the regulation of media ethics. Given the dependence of most media workers on their corporate masters, it is difficult for media professionals to achieve the degree of autonomy which more traditional professions possess. And there are ongoing concerns about the regulation of ownership of the media, with fears that the increasing concentration of media groups places an unhealthy degree of control of public discourse in too few hands and reduces the diversity of voices that is the sign of a vital public sphere. Against the background of these real concerns and difficulties we suggest ways in which, nevertheless, institutional role morality can be promoted in the media, including self-regulatory schemes, codes of ethics, media ombudsmen, and professional educational programs.

Much of this book argues, in effect, that media ethics cannot simply be reduced to the goodness or badness of individual practitioners. Ethics needs to be "designed into" the institution of the media, through the kinds of means indicated in the previous paragraph. Indeed the notion of media ethics is already presupposed in the function of the media: to inform the public truthfully, reliably, credibly, fairly, and in a trustworthy manner. And as we noted earlier, that function has an inbuilt ethical component by virtue of the inherent normative structure of information. One of our primary aims in this book is to disclose and make visible the inherent ethical nature of information and its communication, to which the media as providers of information are necessarily committed.

Nevertheless, ethics is ultimately a matter of individual choice. Over time each of us has internalized a set of attitudes and commitments – a moral character – which we express in our behavior. In Chapter 9, we emphasize the importance of character in governing the behavior of people in the media, given the barriers to other external forms of influence and control. One of the most important influences, for good and bad, on the development of such a character is the people we look up to. An important part of the education of the would-be ethical media practitioner is exposure to, and reflection on, a range of *role models*. In the final chapter of the book we look at a number of journalists whose patterns of professional behavior have led them to be upheld as moral exemplars. This involved their not simply displaying such virtues as bravery, perseverance, and a strong sense of justice, but doing so in such a way as to indicate their understanding of, and commitment to, the animating values of the media – a moral media.

Notes

1. In this book, the term "media" should be understood broadly as referring generally to the mass media, including the "old media" – journalism, advertising, and public relations in newspapers, magazines, radio, and television – and the "new media" including the Internet and mobile phones that still retain to some extent elements of the old media. However different these forms of media may be, they all have in common the essential function of disseminating and communicating information to the public.

References

Kurtz, Howard (2003) N.Y. Times article bears similarities to Texas paper's. *Washington Post*, Apr. 29.

Murrow, Edward R. (1954) A report on Senator Joseph R. McCarthy. *See It Now*. CBS-TV, Mar. 9. http://www.lib.berkeley.edu/MRC/murrowmccarthy.html, accessed Nov. 1, 2010.

New York Times (2003) Times reporter who resigned leaves long trail of deception. May 11.

Further reading

Halberstam, David (1976) CBS: The power and the profits. *Atlantic*. http://www.theatlantic.com/doc/197601/cbs-1, accessed Aug. 31, 2009.

2

Information Ethics as a Guide for the Media: Old Tricks for New Dogs

Introduction

In this chapter we aim to provide a normative framework for the identification, analysis, and evaluation of ethical issues that arise specifically within the media, including new media. "Normative"[1] simply means the general principles that guide and should guide epistemological and ethical conduct. Epistemological conduct generally pertains to matters concerning *knowledge* and involves principles of justification, belief, and truth. Ethical conduct pertains to matters concerning *morality*, both private and public, and involves general principles of harm minimization and increase of the common good as well as respect for people's fundamental rights. The general rationale informing the normative framework that underlies our analyses and evaluations of media ethics throughout this book comprises the following five steps:

Media, Markets, and Morals, First Edition. Edward H. Spence, Andrew Alexandra, Aaron Quinn, and Anne Dunn.
© 2011 Edward H. Spence, Andrew Alexandra, Aaron Quinn, and Anne Dunn. Published 2011 by Blackwell Publishing Ltd.

(1) *Role morality.* If what determines the primary role of a professional practice is its ultimate professional objective(s), then that role determines the ethical rules and principles to which that professional practice is committed. We define the ethical principles, rules, and values to which a professional practice is committed by virtue of its professional role as its role morality. So, for example, the police are, by virtue of their professional role, committed to the principle of justice and the rule of law. The principle of justice and the rule of law, among other things, constitute, therefore, the role morality of policing. Similarly, the media as professional disseminators and communicators of information are committed by their professional role to certain ethical principles of conduct, which as we shall see, include or should include the principles of truthfulness, reliability, objectivity, independence, and trustworthiness, among others.

(2) *Code of ethics.* The role morality of a particular practice, profession, or institution sets, in turn, its own internal rules and codes of conduct for the ethical regulation of that practice, profession, or institution. Thus, typically, the code of ethics of a particular profession, industry, or institution would reflect and be constitutive of the role morality of that profession, industry, or institution. To the extent that a profession's code of ethics does not reflect or is not constitutive of that profession's role morality, that code of ethics is inadequate. It is therefore of paramount importance that before establishing a profession's code of ethics, the role of the profession, determined by the ultimate goals of that profession, is well understood and accurately described. We shall have more to say about the media's code of ethics in Chapter 8.

(3) *Universal public morality.* The role morality of a professional practice, including those of the media, is constrained, however, by the requirements of universal public morality. We define universal public morality simply as the morality which is constituted by principles, rules, and values to which all of us are committed by virtue of being rational human beings and members of the social collective that constitutes civil society. It is based on principles that apply universally to all human agents just by virtue of their

17

common humanity. Those principles are, in turn, justified on the basis of sound rational arguments embedded in contemporary ethical theories,[2] which any reasonable person can accept and ought to accept on the basis of our commonly shared rationality. Thus, for example, deception by the media through disinformation is morally prohibited by universal public morality, even if the "role morality" of a particular medium, such as public relations, for example, sanctions or allows covert deception for maximum persuasion of its media messages. When in conflict, universal public morality as more fundamental and general always trumps role morality since the latter, being a subset of the former, is constrained by it. Taking an extreme example by way of illustration, imagine a professional killer working for the Mafia whose defined role is to kill people for a fee. Even if we could accept that his role of killing people for a fee defined his "role morality" we would hardly accept that as an objectively justified reason for his professional action of killing people. That is because, morally, the killing of people for money is not an acceptable role since it amounts to murder, which contravenes the principles of universal public morality. For universal public morality always takes precedent over any particular professional role morality, whether legal or illegal, when that role is used to violate the legitimate rights and dignity of people, which all of us have simply by virtue of our shared common humanity. Murder or unjustified deception is wrong whether it takes place in China or in the USA.

Universal public morality is *universal* because it applies to everyone without exception in all places at all times under relevantly similar conditions because of our common humanity. Everyone is worthy of moral respect, for example, simply by virtue of being a human being, and likewise, everyone has basic rights to freedom and well-being simply by virtue of being a purposive human agent that requires a basic minimal freedom and well-being to be able to pursue and fulfill his or her individual chosen purposes, so long as those purposes do not violate the legitimate rights of others (Gewirth 1978, 1996; Beyleveld 1991; Spence 2006). Universal public morality is *public* because it applies individually and collectively to members of the general public in their role as citizens both locally and globally. If it were shown, for example, that certain deceptive advertising practices are, according to universal public morality, morally wrong, they would be morally wrong in all places at all times under relevantly similar conditions. So, advertising practices that deceived consumers about the products or services advertised would count as unethical irrespective of the idiosyncratic and specific cultural, social, religious, or political norms of the country in which the deception took place. Such deceptive practices, whether in advertising or other media, would simply be unethical because deceiving people is generally morally wrong since it violates their basic rights to freedom and well-being. Of course the degree of deception which people are prepared to tolerate may vary contextually from culture to culture, from person to person; however, there would be some basic level of deception so harmful that no one would be prepared to tolerate it, regardless of our personal and cultural differences and preferences. For example, a deceptive advertising or marketing message concerning a pharmaceutical product liable to cause death would generally not be tolerated if the consumer's intention of taking that product was to bring about a cure and not death. Thus, generally, media deception at some level that is likely to cause harm would be morally objectionable whether a media consumer lives in China or the USA.

(4) *Ethical commitments from role morality.* By first identifying the primary roles of the media, including those of journalism, advertising, marketing, and public relations, we are then able to determine their respective role moralities and the ethical commitments to which they inevitably give rise. This, in turn, allows us to identify and evaluate specific ethical issues that arise in media practices in relation to the media's specific role moralities.

(5) *Role morality constrained by universal public morality.* Finally, on the basis of universal public morality, we are able to ascertain whether media strategies and practices generally conform to its ethical requirements and prescriptions. If they do not conform, those strategies and practices can in principle be considered ethically unacceptable or at the very least ethically problematic. This is

so even when they appear to conform to the role moralities of their corresponding media industries.

In summary and schematically, the *general normative framework* applied in this book in evaluating ethical issues that arise in the media, is as follows:

> The *roles of the media* determine the *role moralities of the media*, which are constrained by *universal public morality*.

With this general normative framework in place, we can begin to examine what the role of the media is in order to determine if and when the media's role is, in theory and practice, consistent or not consistent with its own role morality, and, more importantly, if and when the media's role is consistent or not consistent with universal public morality. To that end, we shall define the media's role very broadly and generally as simply *the dissemination and communication of information to the public*.

Since the primary and overarching role and business of the media is the dissemination and communication of information to the public,[3] both as citizens and as consumers, it is of crucial importance to first examine and describe what information is. Otherwise, our definition of the role of the media will remain at best vague, at worst obscure. Having offered a definition of information, it is of central importance to an ethical evaluation of the media to then identify the epistemological and ethical commitments to which information itself gives rise, which, in turn, constrain the media as professional providers of information. This process of definition, identification, and evaluation forms the foundation for the whole book and characterizes the novel approach and methodology of the case we make here in *evaluating media ethics on the basis of information ethics*. By information ethics, we simply mean the ethics that are inherently encapsulated within the nature of information itself and arise naturally when information is disseminated and communicated. In a sense, information has its own inherent role morality that both empowers and constrains the conduct of its disseminators and communicators. This is the topic discussed in detail in the next section.

20

Good media practices generally, and good journalism specifically, are based and to some extent thrive on a diversity of perspectives from those who supply information and informed opinions to the public. In this respect, new media journalism is a contemporary newsgathering and disseminating method with enormous communication potential. It is composed of an online forum that can connect a great number of diverse contributors and audiences from different communities, countries, and continents. In this context, the contributions of nonprofessionals via the phenomenon known as "citizen journalism" or "user-created content" – performed on a global level through the World Wide Web – is a potential contemporary marvel because of its wide reach and range of diversity. People can now access information worldwide on any topic at any time at the touch of a computer key, or of an icon on their smart phones. They can upload text and images and share it with people around the globe in an instant. They can access and use information to check the weather, make travel plans, buy and sell any number of products, both real and virtual – fancy an Armani suit for your avatar in Second Life? A few hundred Linden dollars will buy you one – and post comments and information on hotels and restaurants they visited. The downside, of course, is that the deregulation of the Internet has its own problems and pitfalls. Can we always trust the veracity, credibility, and reliability of the sources of the information we access on the World Wide Web? Whom can we trust and why? Who provides an authoritative quality control of Internet information, one that we can trust?

Although this chapter will to some extent focus on new media and in particular on new media journalism, the arguments put forward are also relevant to all media, including those of journalism (broadcast and print), advertising, marketing, and public relations, both offline and online. This is because information as the single underlying source of the ethical commitments that both constrains and empowers the media is common to both the "old media" and the "new media." If there are differences between the two they can be explained in terms of the different ways in which information is produced, disseminated, and used.

21

In summary our aims in this chapter are to:

- provide an argument to show why information has a dual normative structure with regard to its practical applications (creation, production, dissemination, communication, and consumption) which morally binds all communicators of information, and especially media communicators, focusing generally on all information and particularly on digital information disseminated on the Internet;
- provide an analysis to demonstrate that the ethical and epistemological principles and standards to which the dual normative structure of information commits the media by virtue of its general role as disseminator and communicator of information are universal and global;
- identify and examine the ethical obstacles presented by different beliefs among different cultures to the thesis supported in this book, namely, that the ethical commitments that bind the media are universal. We can for convenience refer to this thesis as a *global information ethics*. We shall do so by focusing on a distinction between *thin* and *thick* moral values and the role they play with regard to supporting our thesis for a global information and media ethics.

The Normative Structure of Informational Action

As we saw above, while universal public morality applies to all human agents, what we have called role morality applies to those who occupy specific roles.[4] Although role morality is narrower in its scope, it is constrained by universal public morality and must be consistent with it. In this section, we look in more detail at the role morality of the media, that is, morality as it applies to people by virtue of their work in the media. Thus, in order to understand that morality we need to understand the ends (that is, the purposes) of the media.

As we stated above, the ultimate end of the media is to provide information. The provision of information is, of course, a normal, and indeed fundamental, part of our ordinary dealings with each other. We each rely on other people to provide us with all sorts of information, ranging from everyday things like what we are having for dinner, to matters of vital importance, such as whether a medical test has shown that we are suffering from a fatal condition. Information, then, is knowledge codified in a form which makes it available to others. So understood, information is a public phenomenon. Information as a public phenomenon is in keeping with one of the fundamental principles of journalism: the dissemination of information to the public on matters of public interest. Furthermore, it is the public's right to receive information on matters of public interest – the right to know – which endows journalism and the media generally with the right to *freedom of the press*. As we shall see in Chapter 3, the right to freedom of the press and its basis for justification on the right of the public to know is what distinguishes the media as a business from other merely commercial businesses.

The provision of information has what we call an *inherent normative structure*: those who claim to be providing others with information are in virtue of that claim obliged to behave in certain ways. Before looking at the detail of this structure, we should note two implications of characterizing information as knowledge codified in a form which makes it available to others. First, it implies that there is a relationship between provider and receiver as, at least implicitly, information is always targeted at a potential audience. This relationship generates duties and rights for both audience and producer. Second, it implies that since information is a type of knowledge both provider and receiver of the information must be aiming at the truth. Knowledge involves belief. But knowledge is more than belief, since we have false beliefs which cannot be counted as knowledge. So knowledge is, at least, true belief. For something to count as information then, it must be true or at least truthful. We shall say more about the distinction between "true information" and "truthful information" below. If information is not true it is not information but rather misinformation or disinformation.[5] Truth and truthfulness are therefore at the heart of the inherent normative structure of information which governs the exchange of information. It is only if information providers are dedicated to the discovery of the truth and to providing it in an accurate and comprehensible way to others that information will in fact be generated and transmitted.

The role of the media as disseminator and communicator of information can therefore be evaluated more specifically on the basis of what we identify in this chapter as the dual normative structure of informational action and the epistemological and ethical norms (hence "normative") to which information commits all media practitioners in their capacity of informational agents. Using the dual obligation information theory (DOIT) model developed by Spence (2007–2009a, 2009b, 2009c) we now demonstrate that media practitioners are committed to ethical norms in a twofold manner simply because the dual obligation information theory model comprises two main parts that together show that information as communicative action is doubly normative (Spence 2007–2009a, 2009b, 2009c).

(1) Information has an inherent normative structure that commits its producers, communicators, and users, in fact everyone who deals with information, to certain mandatory epistemological and ethical commitments. Briefly, the argument for the inherent normative structure of information is as follows: if information is a type of knowledge (it must be capable of yielding knowledge; one must be able to learn from it) it must comply with the epistemological conditions of knowledge, specifically, that of truth. And if the dissemination of information is based on the justified and rightful expectation among its disseminators and especially its users that such information meet the minimal condition of truth, then the disseminators of information are committed to certain widely recognized and accepted epistemological criteria. Those epistemic criteria comprise, in the main, objectivity as well as the independence, reliability, accuracy, and trustworthiness of the sources that generate the information. The epistemology of information, in turn, commits its disseminators to certain ethical principles and values, such as honesty, sincerity, truthfulness, trustworthiness, and reliability (also epistemological values), and fairness, including justice, which requires the equal distribution of the informational goods to all citizens. Hence, in terms of its dissemination, information has an

24

intrinsic normative structure that commits everyone involved in its creation, production, search, communication, and consumption to epistemological and ethical norms and these norms being intrinsic to the normative structure of information are rationally unavoidable and thus not merely optional.

(2) The negligent or purposeful abuse of information in violation of the epistemological and ethical commitments to which its inherent normative structure gives rise is also a violation of universal rights – specifically, universal rights to freedom and well-being to which all agents are entitled by virtue of simply being agents, and in particular informational agents that routinely engage in informational action. The goal of this argument is to show that, apart from committing its disseminators to unavoidable epistemological and ethical standards by virtue of its own inherent normative structure, information commits its disseminators to respect for people's rights in virtue of the inherent normative structure of action. That is, information must not be disseminated in ways that violate people's fundamental rights to freedom and well-being, individually or collectively, or undermine their capacity for self-fulfillment (negative rights) when they engage, as they routinely do, in informational action, that is, engage in the dissemination and communication of information both as transmitters and as receivers. In addition, information must as far as possible be disseminated in ways that secure and promote people's generic rights and capacity for self-fulfillment (positive rights) when those rights cannot be secured or promoted by the individuals themselves and can be so secured and promoted at no comparable cost to its disseminators. The argument outlined above is based on Alan Gewirth's principle of generic consistency (PGC), which offers a description and prescription for both the rational authority (based primarily on instrumental and deductive rationality) and the content of the fundamental rights (freedom and well-being) that persons have necessarily and only by virtue (sufficient reason) of being purposive and active agents.[6]

Hence, the abuse of information through, for example, disinformation practices, constitutes (1) a violation of the epistemological and ethical commitments to which the inherent normative structure of *information* itself gives rise and (2) a violation of universal rights to freedom and well-being that the inherent normative structure of *action* gives rise and to which all agents, and specifically informational agents, are entitled. Echoing Umberto Eco's claim in *The Open Work* (1989, 66) that with regard to human beings information theory becomes communication theory – this chapter shows that the demonstrated dual normative structure of information in terms of its own inherent normative structure, as well as the universal rights of informational agents to which information as informational action gives rise, confirms and supports Eco's claim. Moreover, the ethical and epistemological commitment that binds the media in this twofold manner is universal and global. However, because of the obvious cultural diversity that exists between countries, we will examine a bit later in the chapter whether these cultural diversities can be accommodated and accounted for within the universal and global ethical model proposed in this chapter.

In providing the dual normative model for the evaluation of information outlined above, the chapter employs an epistemological account of information based on a minimal nuclear definition of information. Following Luciano Floridi it defines information as "well formed meaningful data that is truthful" (2005), and following Fred Dretske it defines information as "an objective commodity capable of yielding knowledge," knowledge in turn defined as "information caused belief" (1999, 44–45 and 86).

As we briefly indicated above, what is necessary for both information and knowledge is *truth*. For information without truth is not strictly speaking information but either misinformation (the unintentional dissemination of well-formed and meaningful false data) or disinformation (the intentional dissemination of false "information"). Of course, journalists, for example, both offline and online, cannot always know with certainty whether the information they disseminate is true or not. However, in such cases, they should at least have a reasonable justified belief, responsive to at least some minimal objective verification capable of sustaining that belief that the information they disseminate is probably if not certainly true.

One could make the case, for example, that the dissemination of "information" by journalists concerning the claim that Iraq possessed weapons of mass destruction before the start of the war in Iraq was not based on a reasonable, justified belief capable of yielding knowledge. Insofar as this was the case, the dissemination of such "information" was misinformation at best, disinformation at worst.

Examination of the inherent normative structure of information and its role morality has helped us, in turn, to understand the general morality of the media. That is, the dissemination of true or truthful information to the public. That morality becomes particularly demanding because of the importance of the media's role as providers of information to modern societies in an age characterized as the Age of Information. If people are misinformed by the media, or unable to gain easy access to it, their vital interests are likely to be harmed and their rights violated. Hence, the provision of information to all members of society through the media can be seen a matter of justice.

Looking more closely at the dissemination of information by the media we can distinguish at least four distinct processes involved in the provision of information:

- *evidence gathering* and assessment;
- the *codification of knowledge* gained through that process, that is, its transformation into information;
- the *transmission* of that information to others; and
- the *acceptance* of the information by those others.

The first two processes involve the provider[7] alone, the third involves both the provider and the recipient of information, and the last involves the recipient alone. In each of these processes there are normative demands on information providers. The process of the evidence gathering, for instance, obviously needs to be oriented to the discovery of the truth. This requires *objectivity* – the ability to give conflicting evidence its due weight, without being influenced by personal preferences or prejudice – as well as the capacity to gather and analyze relevant evidence. It also entails *diligence* – the requirement that all relevant evidence is gathered and assessed, and that all feasible hypotheses which make sense of that evidence are considered. Depending on the nature of the subject matter, evidence gathering may require specialized skills and equipment. At the very least it requires the ability to follow and construct chains of reasoning. Some of the most difficult issues in media ethics arise at this stage owing to the potential for conflict between the demand for diligence and the constraints on behavior imposed by universal public morality. For instance, we all have a duty to respect each other's privacy. This duty imposes constraints on the kinds of methods which can be used to gain information, such as eaves-dropping on family conversations, even where matters of genuine public importance are being discussed, and where there is no other way of gaining this information.[8] (The same point holds for methods such as deception or intimidation.)

Even when someone has the capacity to gather and assess evidence they may be rendered unable to do so by elements of their personality or the context within which they operate. Consider a climate scientist who depends on a coalmining company to fund their research. The climate scientist is well trained in scientific method and has the capacity to assess evidence about climate change. Nevertheless, his findings may appear to lack *independence*, that is, to be unduly influenced by the interests of others in assessing evidence or presenting findings. Independence thus is a precondition for objectivity. On the other hand, even when independence is assured some choose to tell the truth only when they judge that it suits them to do so, or are simply cavalier with the truth – they make emphatic assertions about things they are not sure of; they do not check their facts, though it is easy to do so; and so on. They will be perceived as lacking *reliability*.

The codification process requires the information provider to present the knowledge gained in the evidence gathering stage in a form that accurately reflects what was found, and does so in a way that is likely to be understandable to the target audience. The two main requirements at this stage, then, would seem to be *accuracy* and *accessibility*. There is often a tension between these two demands. It may be very difficult, for example, to present information about some complex matter of public interest to an audience which possesses little relevant expertise, and has a limited tolerance for involved explanations, or even for qualifications of claims. While there are no hard and fast rules in this area with regard to some concession for the sake of accessibility, there is a variety of means that can be used to reduce the need to make such concessions.

The transmission process requires that information be not only presented in a form that is accessible to its target audience, but made physically available to that audience. This is one of the points at which matters of justice come into play: given the importance of access to media in modern societies, the provision of such access is necessary and just.

The final stage in provision of information involves its acceptance by its target audience. In our ordinary dealings with each other there is a general presumption of trustworthiness. If someone tells us something, it is reasonable to believe what they tell us, unless there is a good reason to think that they are unable to know the truth. Among these reasons is lack of what we have identified above as objectivity, diligence, independence, and reliability. Note that even if someone actually is in possession of the truth and attempts to communicate it to others, their attempt will fail if those others see the communicator as unreliable or lacking in independence.

We have outlined here considerations relevant to how media workers and organizations *should* behave based on the inherent normative structure of information. These considerations at least implicitly if not explicitly inform media practice. A good deal of the training of media practitioners, for example, focuses on methods for ensuring the accuracy of information presented. Media outlets have mechanisms for acknowledging and redressing inaccuracies, and so on. At least, this is true for what is now being called "traditional media," by contrast to "new media." In the next section we look at some of the problems generated by the rise of the new media.

New Media, New Ethical Issues?

The term "new media" applies to the plethora of new technological devices, such as camcorders, laptops, cell phones, computer networks, and the like, which have opened up new possibilities for the gathering and transmission of information, as well as to organizations which are defined by their use of these devices for the presentation of information. The line between the new media and traditional media is admittedly blurred. The many mainstream newspapers that have settled online, for instance, differ only in a minor way from the physical newspaper: traditional text- and photo-based reporting in a new medium – the World Wide Web. Some others have offered video and audio in addition to the traditional text and picture methods of newspaper production. Still, the new technology is clearly providing major challenges to traditional media organizations, affecting the way in which information is gathered, processed, and consumed. Web logs (blogs), for example, serve a wide variety of traditional and nontraditional news purposes and allow audience interaction both to debate and to augment the original report in a way which has never been possible before. In this way, the distinction between provider and consumer of information begins to break down. Additionally, consider how small, portable electronic devices such as camcorders and cell phones allow journalists to capture and disseminate news in ways that traditional newsgathering methods sometimes cannot. And this is perhaps only the tip of the iceberg in relation to independent newsgathering using portable technology.

The presence of these many and diverse new media has given rise to much debate in media criticism and media ethics scholarship as to whether there needs to be a new media ethics, as distinct from the ethics that has applied to traditional media. In our view, although the rise of the new media has certainly created particular problems, there is a common framework between old and new, deriving from the inherent normative structure of information and its communication. We aim to show this commonality by focusing on some of the problems that appear to beset the new media.

One matter that seems to stand out in new media ethics discourse is the difficulty of quality control. Getting the news first – a longstanding high-stakes competition among traditional news market competitors – has become increasingly worrisome given the real-time speed of Web publishing: reports can be uploaded to the Web nearly instantly as news unfolds, but without safeguards such as copy-editing and fact checking. The haste with which many news-gatherers post their reports on the Web naturally challenges our confidence in the accuracy and completeness of their coverage. In these cases, the worry is often that competition drives the rate at which one publishes rather than the confidence reporters and editors have in the completeness and accuracy of their stories. In terms of the normative structure of information requirement, the use of new media is adversely affecting the reliability of the information providers.

Outside of mainstream media, another matter regarding quality concerns the question of who is reporting and publishing the news. "The Internet is particularly affecting journalism in terms of its credibility (or lack thereof) in an anonymous global communications environment where everyone is both producer and consumer of content" (Deuze and Yeshua 2001, 274). With the advent of blogging, this concern has only increased because the process of publishing has become even easier (more automated) than publishing a web page, and even more so than a physical newspaper. Thus, many potential news-gatherers who have not been trained in journalism and indoctrinated with its standards for objectivity and diligence, among other professional values, have the ability to report and publish widely. Though it is unfair to assume that citizen journalists are not ethically motivated or at least adequately ethically motivated, it is good to be skeptical of their awareness of reporting standards and the degree to which even unintended variances from these standards can affect the social well-being of news audiences and their communities.

However, there are also instances in which citizen journalists are responsible for more overt ethical indiscretions than mere ignorance of journalistic standards. For example, an online citizen journalism forum hosted by the *Rocky Mountain News* called *YourHub* was used at least once to plant disguised press releases for political candidates (Brown 2006; McBride 2006). In such cases, we have a failure of independence (one of the conditions for objectivity). As Poynter Institute for Media Studies ethicist Kelly McBride (2006) criticizes, "In this media saturated world, in this era of viral marketing, how's the average consumer supposed to know the difference between real journalism and a cleverly disguised press release or a marketing campaign? We could start by labeling them as such." Therefore, whether it is mere ignorance of journalistic standards that does damage or an act of undermining these standards, citizen journalists can pose a substantial threat to the credibility of journalism and its intended effects.

That said, the emergence of web-based journalism and citizen journalism is not by any means only bad news. The Web offers journalists a way to better inform people and offers audiences a better way to be informed because of the centralized nature of the medium: go online and you can read the local newspaper in Des Moines, hear an audio broadcast (or podcast) from Melbourne, and watch a video from Hong Kong. Thus, the Web offers a wide set of cross-cultural news perspectives – either mainstream or citizen-based – in one easily accessible medium. Moreover, the very profusion of available news channels would seem to provide the potential for some kind of self-correcting mechanism, where falsity is likely to become apparent by virtue of its inconsistency with most of other reports.[9]

The public can also reap great rewards from citizen journalism despite its aforementioned threat to journalistic standards. For example, recent political violence in both Fiji and Myanmar was largely documented first if not best by ordinary citizens (Drash 2007). Some of the first pictures in Western news outlets of violence against Myanmar's Buddhist monks were sent by cellular phone from ordinary citizens when most Western journalists were barred from entering the country. Moreover, anonymous bloggers were among the most impartial in reporting about Fiji's 2006 coups, when rampant self-censorship spurred by fear of the new regime plagued the country's journalists (Foster 2007). In the absence of new technology and its newborn citizen journalists, there would be greater difficulty establishing a wide international and even domestic awareness of various socially important news stories.

The Normative Transition from Right to Good: From Thin to Thick

Our goal so far has been to offer an argument that commits disseminators of information – including new media journalists – to universal and global ethical behavior regardless of the variety and differences of their cultures. We were able to demonstrate this in the form of a "thin" theory – the dual obligation information theory ("thin" theories use a minimal and abstract logical structure that appeals for its conceptual authority to our common and shared human rationality), by arguing that: (1) the inherent normative structure of information itself commits its disseminators to universal and unavoidable epistemological and ethical standards that relate to information; and (2) demonstrating that disseminators of information engaged in informational action, both as transmitters and as receivers of information, are also committed by their own intrinsic rational agency to respecting the universal rights to freedom and well-being of all other informational agents.

This was possible because what all rational humans have in common – a minimal natural need and necessity to act purposively as agents, and as informational agents specifically – exists independently of cultural influences. The conclusion of the argument from the dual normativity of information based on the dual obligation information theory (DOIT) was that the ethical dissemination of information

33

requires the truthful dissemination and communication of information as well as respect for the rights of all informational agents. Moreover, it requires the inculcation of virtues of character and the cultivation of moral sentiments as enabling dispositions for complying with those rights and, importantly, for the attainment of self-fulfillment and a good life for oneself and for others.[10]

Although that argument addressed implicitly and very broadly the role of the good and the good life for people generally in relation to what is morally right by reference to information and informational action, it is also necessary to examine specific informational goods in more detail and in particular with regard to the influence different cultures may have on such "thick" concepts as the virtues of truthfulness, honesty, sincerity, justice, freedom, and so on. These concepts are called "thick" because they are concepts about which (1) people typically have a grasp, and (2) people typically have experience and thus some emotional or tangible attachment (Spence and Quinn 2008).

It is important to note that there are strong arguments for the intrinsic or objective value of virtues such as truthfulness, honesty, sincerity, justice, and so on. Similarly, there are many philosophers who argue that there are objective or universal values held in kind by all humans. Isaiah Berlin (1958), for example, articulated an idea called "value pluralism" in which he claimed there are at least some objective human values. For Berlin, the foremost objective human value is liberty. Since this early work many more philosophers and political theorists have supported or articulated some form of objective value pluralism.

Martha Nussbaum (1986), Michael Walzer (1995), Joseph Raz (1999), Bernard Williams (1981, 1985) and Michael Stocker (1990) among many others offer, or at least acknowledge, a core set of values that they contend all humans hold. Typically, the source of justification for this belief is genealogical, based in natural law, or, as with the principle of generic consistency (PGC) earlier, based in human rationality and agency. Thus, it is argued by many value pluralists that objective values exist because humans have demonstrated their possession of these values throughout recorded human history, or because they require them in order to survive as a species (Mason 2006).

However, despite their inherent goodness, the way in which they are conceived in practice does, on occasion, differ from culture to culture. To clarify this point, we contend that all cultures necessarily have a conception of justice, truthfulness, integrity, and so on (often illustrated by the convergence if not consensus one finds in, for example, professional codes of ethics) through which they understand what is just and truthful and what constitutes integrity. However, the specific ways in which cultures apply justice in particular situations may differ. For example, capital punishment may be considered just in the United States but unjust in the Netherlands, or, to the contrary, euthanasia may largely be considered unjust in the United States, but just in the Netherlands.

How is it, then, that objectively good virtues or values can be seen differently? To understand this, we must understand the concept of reasonable moral disagreement – that is, that there is in some cases more than one good solution to a specific moral problem. For example, how should a society punish someone who has murdered? In these cases, and with the solutions that have been offered, there might be good reasons for reaching a conclusion either to support or to reject capital punishment or euthanasia – reasons that any rational person could justifiably hold.

However, reasonable moral disagreement cannot account for some cultural differences, such as genocide and anti-Semitism in Nazi Germany, or the spread of disinformation through omission or commission by governments in an attempt to exercise a dictatorial control over its citizens, as in the present case in Myanmar. There are simply no good moral reasons for such actions; instead they result from concepts (which we cannot cover comprehensively in this chapter) such as evil or self-deception or some combination thereof. Therefore, what we must now examine is which of these objective "goods" – governed by reason – are most crucial for new media journalists to possess.

Key Goods in the Media and New Media Journalism

Truthfulness is a complex and contentious concept. It is also a foundational moral value for journalists. Therefore, it is crucial that we carefully argue its strength as an objective good. In *Truth and Truthfulness* (2002), Bernard Williams sought to argue against various thinkers who doubt the existence of objective truth – that is, the position that truth does invariably exist in a way cognitively accessible to humans. Thus, Williams argues, the values of truth and truthfulness, and their corresponding virtues – *sincerity* and *accuracy* – are indispensable to the human social world (see also Chapter 4). These virtues, Williams claims, will continue in human society "in something like the more courageous, intransigent, and socially effective forms that they have acquired over their history . . . and that the ways in which future people will come to make sense of things will enable them to see the truth and not be broken by it" (2002, 269).

What Williams offers us in this weaker understanding of truth is similar to the way we often wish to conceive of truth in the media and particularly in journalism, what Williams refers to as sincerity and accuracy. Note, however, that Williams's account of truth is weaker only in the sense that it is more commonplace than other more metaphysically ambitious and demanding philosophical notions of truth. Thus accuracy and truth are uncontroversially compatible (truth could not be inaccurate and accuracy could not be false) with regard to a definition of information that underlies and is implied by this chapter: namely, an objective commodity capable of yielding knowledge or, if you prefer, accurate facts ("accurate" is redundant here and is used merely rhetorically for emphasis). And since by definition knowledge must be true so must information. Information must at least be truthful, that is, its dissemination must be intended to yield truth, even if in some cases, through no fault of the disseminator, it fails to do so.

First, it is ideal and desirable for media practitioners and journalists in particular to be *accurate* and *truthful* in their recounting of facts and potentially nonfactual claims insofar as they can pursue and procure verification in support of those claims. Second, journalists and media practitioners must be *sincere*, which primarily concerns the intentions of a speaker. To better understand this, it is useful to expand these concepts by appealing to epistemology, because in many cases there are strong interrelationships between knowledge and truth (and the concept of information illustrates this), as a widely acknowledged (though still contentious) definition of knowledge is justified *true* belief (David 2005). Though journalists do not always deal directly with knowledge, because of the often unverifiable data with which they work, there must be epistemic standards to help journalists determine what information is newsworthy with regard to truth, knowledge, or some other epistemic measurement. Journalists have a tendency to call this approach to justification *objectivity*, which relies on certain forms of verifiability and/or accuracy. Thus, although newsworthy information needn't be knowledge per se, what epistemic standards must it meet to be newsworthy?

One possibility is to bracket off the "truth" condition from the definition of knowledge, so that we're left with this alternative epistemic standard, *justified belief*, which maintains its dedication to sincerity and accuracy. Although a justified belief does lose epistemic value by losing truth (the philosophically stern kind) as a necessary condition, it can nonetheless retain substantial informational value. For, although beliefs can be held for a variety of reasons – both good reasons and bad reasons – justified beliefs must, at least, meet a set of justificatory criteria, whatever they may be in a given domain. In the domain of news, because there are regularly instances in which something potentially less than knowledge is still publicly important, there must be justificatory criteria for publishing information partly based on whether the information is worth believing. And this can be achieved on the basis that the information disseminated is supported by reasonable but incomplete evidence sufficient at least for arriving at a justified opinion that the information is probably true; that is, it must be sincere and accurate within the means of verification available to the journalist at the time. Given the definition of information we offered, such "information" can be conceived only as potential or provisional information. So what are some possible justificatory criteria for evaluating "information" that is not necessarily sufficient for knowledge because its truth is uncertain?

Several scholars have weighed in on this matter in the area of social epistemology, focusing particularly on the justification for beliefs regarding social phenomena. In this literature, there is a distinction relevant to the aforementioned justification issue in journalism. As Goldman (2001) claims, there are *basic* sources of justification for holding beliefs such as perception, memory, or inductive inference. These sources are generally held as the more reliable type, such as when one witnesses an event at first hand. However, there are also *derivative* sources of justification, such as when Person A listens to Person B's testimony, like the example of a journalist who hears George Bush's evaluation of the Iraq war. In such cases, we cannot be certain that what Bush says is truthful, but we can be certain about what Bush said. Because journalism must often rely on derivative sources of testimony for news, how then do we best evaluate derivative sources of information as newsworthy?

The first instance is somewhat arbitrary in that journalists are to some extent powerless to ignore some testifiers merely because of their political or social influence – presidents, governors, mayors, and other holders of high office. The justification for publishing their words rests more in the legitimacy of a representative democracy: voters have endowed them with news legitimacy. A second instance is also potentially epistemically weak in that one's testimony may become relevant as a matter of luck – a lone bystander to a publicly important event would make that person's testimony relevant regardless, to some extent, of that person's other traits. The person simply had access to information that no one else had and must be (carefully) relied upon to provide their testimony.

The third instance, however, is much stronger epistemically, because it requires us to ask whether certain traits of a testifier (e.g., their trustworthiness) and/or the quality of their testimony provide a justification for our subscribing to a belief that they espouse. Thus, one proposition about the justificatory value of testimony, called *reductionism*, is the claim that "a hearer H is justified or warranted in accepting a speaker's report or factual statement only if *H* is justified in believing that the speaker is reliable and sincere, where the latter justification rests on sources other than the testimony itself" (Goldman 2001).

Truth and truthfulness in citizen journalism

As we claimed, truthfulness – a commitment to speaking the truth – is at the heart of the inherent normative structure which governs information provision. Let us consider a well-known case involving both mainstream journalists and citizen journalism in the light of this commitment.

Rathergate

In 2004 Dan Rather claimed on the TV news series *60 Minutes* that US President George W. Bush failed to fulfill his military service. That claim was based on a report that was apparently made by one of Bush's supervising officers in 1972 (Gahran 2005).

Almost immediately after the show aired, a citizen journalist with the username "Buckhead" posted a thread on a conservative discussion forum called *Free Republic* alleging that the document Rather used to support his story was a forgery. The citizen journalist, who was later identified as Atlanta attorney Harry McDougald, prompted a string of subsequent blogs that made similar claims about the authenticity of the documents. CBS eventually apologized for the apparent error (the authenticity of the original report has been neither proved nor disproved) and Rather left his position with CBS. However, numerous media critics – in addition to their shaming of Rather and CBS – also criticized several bloggers who prematurely concluded that the documents were false (Pein 2005). In its investigation of Rather's apparently faulty report the *Columbia Journalism Review* published an article scolding bloggers for committing many of the same indiscretions as Rather.

Dan Rather and company stand accused of undue haste, carelessness, excessive credulity, and, in some minds, partisanship, in what has become known as "Memogate." But CBS's critics are guilty of many of the very same sins. First, much of the bloggers' vaunted fact-checking was seriously warped. Their driving assumptions were often drawn from flawed information or based on faulty logic. Personal attacks passed for analysis. Second, and worse, the reviled MSM often followed the bloggers' lead. As mainstream media critics of CBS piled on, rumors shaped the news and conventions of sourcing and skepticism fell by the wayside. (Pein 2005)

In this case one can see both sides of the citizen journalism debate. It appears that Rather hastily presented the Bush story to news audiences without thoroughly checking the authenticity of the documents (thus giving victory to citizen journalists acting as watchdogs by discrediting a popular mainstream journalist). However, the citizen journalists in this case were guilty of similar indiscretions; by hastily reporting Rather's errors prior to having sufficient evidence or testimony to disprove his report, citizen journalists not only were involved in an instance of moral self-contradiction, but perpetuated the credibility problem that plagues citizen journalist more generally. If both parties had better inculcated and implemented the value of truthfulness, including the values of objectivity and diligence, they would most likely have made fewer errors and produced a more accurate report. Both Rather and "Buckhead," and subsequent bloggers, could and should have sought stronger evidence and testimony to support their claims. For, if the truthfulness of a document can so quickly and easily come into question, and counter-evidence cannot be offered by CBS to support the authenticity of the documents, it is likely that very little fact checking was performed by CBS prior to the airing of *60 Minutes*. Moreover, in the rapid response of "Buckhead," supported by virtually no evidence – only mere conjecture – McDougald also showed poor judgment in relation to offering truthful news. This lack of truth, and of necessary supporting evidence to at least demonstrate the likelihood of it being true, automatically negates its status as information as we have defined it, since truth (or sufficient truthfulness) is by definition a necessary condition of information.

Justice as a guide to media

Having described the various truth-related values above, we must now describe yet another crucial virtue for media practitioners and journalists in particular, that of justice. The virtue of justice has been conceived primarily in terms of a principle of impartiality which frames our reasons and justifications in universal terms. So conceived, it plays a central role regarding matters of social well-being and fairness. Plato and Aristotle understood justice as a virtue that penetrated more or less all matters of morality. Justice in this sense promotes that persons, entities, or things generally ought to be handled according to how they deserve to be treated (Dahl 1991).

One could imagine the necessity of justice as a central good for new media journalists because of its ability to promote fairness as a crucial component of one's journalistic conscientiousness. The dual obligation information theory, as we saw earlier, supports and prescribes respect for the equal rights of all informational agents, specifically, rights to freedom and well-being.

A violation of justice is evident in the Rathergate case, not just by Rather but also the citizen journalists involved. Rather and his CBS team appear to have shown a lack of respect for the basic informational rights of their audiences to freedom and well-being. More specifically, those foundational justice-based rights were violated by presenting a poorly researched report which, in principle, is a violation of audiences' autonomous agency. In practice, this often leads to substantial social consequences that occur when misinformed people make poor decisions as a direct result of the misinformation presented by journalists.

Conclusion

Our aim in this chapter has been to provide an argument for a universal and global media ethics derived from a universal and global information ethics that guides the dissemination of information as it applies to the media generally and to new media specifically, including new media journalism. To this end, we offered an account of the *right* to information (rights to freedom and well-being) which all informational agents have by virtue of the dual normativity of information, and a complementary account of the *good* – a set of virtues, values, and moral sentiments designed to guide moral action – relevant and suitable to the media, including new media. What our analysis provides is a duality of rational arguments that commits all media disseminators to universal ethical principles and values through the normative structure of information as well as the normative structure of action that supports rights to freedom and well-being. Together, those rational arguments prescribe that all informational agents, including media disseminators of information, must act rightly and virtuously with regard to one's informational practices and the moral obligations to which they give rise.

Adding a morally thick account of the good, with which most people are familiar, to a thin notion offered on the basis of the dual obligation information theory bolsters the motivational muscle of the theoretical commitment to the universal and global principles we have argued for in this chapter. By doing so, we hope to have given a more compelling account for motivating moral behavior. Of course neither notions of the right nor of the good can completely eliminate confusion brought about by contextual nuance, or eliminate all conceptual and semantic confusion from ethical deliberation. However, they do provide a rational theoretical framework that offers practical substantive standards to guide members of any culture to act rightly and virtuously with regard to their informational practices. This rational and ethical theoretical framework provides a foundational and tangible argument for universal ethical and virtuous behavior among all disseminators of information including both the traditional and new media in an age where information, owing to its digitization and the Internet, is increasingly becoming global, in an age rightly described as the Age of Information.

Chapter study questions

1. What is role morality and why is it relevant to the professions generally and to the media specifically?

2. Do different media institutions such as journalism, public relations, and advertising have the same or different role moralities? Describe the role moralities of these three media institutions.

3. What is the one fundamental goal or role that all media institutions, both old and new, have in common?

4. What are the epistemological and ethical commitments that naturally arise out of the essential characteristics of information in the process of its communication?

5. Are the epistemological and ethical commitments that arise naturally from within the essential structure of information universal and thus global, or merely local? Are they constrained by the specific cultural, religious, social, and political institutions of different counties? Are these differences compatible or incompatible with the universality thesis of information proposed in this chapter? Give reasons for supporting either position.

6. Are the institutional role moralities of the different media, such as journalism, public relations, and advertising, always compatible, at least in theory, with universal public morality? Do they come into conflict, if at all, because (a) the role moralities of those media institutions are in theory incompatible with universal public morality, or (b) even though the role moralities of those media institutions are compatible with universal public morality in theory, they can nevertheless become incompatible with universal public morality in cases where some of the practices of those media institutions deviate from universal public morality.

7. Why should universal public morality always take precedence over the role moralities of the media?

8. Do the epistemological and ethical commitments that emanate from the essential structure of information also apply to the dissemination of information on the Internet?

Notes

1. "Normative" is an *evaluative* term used throughout this book to describe collectively the principles, rules, and values that ethically

and epistemologically ought to guide our conduct by *prescribing* how we should behave in relation to others, both personally and professionally. In other words, "normative" is a term that describes and prescribes the things we ought to do and the things we ought to avoid doing. A normative framework is therefore an ethical roadmap which provides our actions with ethical direction. Moreover, it provides us with a *method* for ethically evaluating the rightness and wrongness of our actions, both personally and professionally.

2. For a comprehensive and helpful exposition and critical comparative analysis of contemporary ethical theories see Boylan (2000).

3. We shall examine in Chapter 5 some of the more specific roles of the media, such as the respective roles of journalism, advertising and marketing, and public relations. However different the specific roles of those media might be, their overarching and general role remains the same: namely, the dissemination and communication of information to the public, comprising both citizens and consumers.

4. For a more in-depth and detailed discussion of the normative structure of information see Spence (2007, 2009a, 2009b).

5. Note that some information is a record of claims or opinions. Much of the information presented in the media is of this form. Such claims may be false and known to be false. Moreover, it is arguable as to whether opinion as such (e.g., whether it would be better for a country to have a conservative or a progressive government) can be true or false. Nevertheless, the status of these things as (potential) information is not jeopardized by the fact that they are not true. In 2003 US Secretary of State Colin Powell made a number of false claims about the existence of weapons of mass destruction in his speech to the UN. Media outlets which uncritically retailed those claims misled their audiences, but those which reported that Powell had made the claims gave their audience some true information about what Powell had said.

6. The universal entitlement to universal rights to freedom and well-being by all human agents is based on the argument for the principle of generic consistency (PGC) by the American philosopher Alan Gewirth. For a detailed discussion and defense of that argument see Gewirth (1978–1998); Beyleveld (1991); and Spence (2006). In brief, Gewirth's main thesis is that every rational agent, in virtue of engaging in action, is logically committed to accept a supreme moral

principle, the principle of generic consistency. The basis of his thesis is found in his doctrine that action has a normative structure, and because of this structure every rational agent, just in virtue of being an agent, is committed to certain necessary prudential and moral constraints.Gewirth undertakes to prove his claim that every agent, qua agent, is committed to certain prudential and moral constraints in virtue of the normative structure of action in three main stages. First, he undertakes to show that by virtue of engaging in voluntary and purposive action, every agent makes certain implicitly evaluative judgments about the goodness of his purposes, and hence about the necessary goodness of his freedom and well-being, which are the necessary conditions for the fulfillment of his purposes. Second, he undertakes to show that by virtue of the necessary goodness which an agent attaches to his freedom and well-being, the agent implicitly claims that he has rights to these. At this stage of the argument, these rights being merely self-regarding are only prudential rights. Third, Gewirth undertakes to show that every agent must claim these rights in virtue of the sufficient reason that he is a *prospective purposive agent* (PPA) who has purposes he wants to fulfill. Furthermore, every agent must accept that, since he has rights to his freedom and well-being for the sufficient reason that he is a PPA, he is logically committed, on pain of self-contradiction, to also accept the rational generalization that all PPAs have rights to freedom and well-being. At this third stage of the argument these rights, being not only self-regarding but also other-regarding, are now moral rights. The conclusion of Gewirth's argument for the PGC is in fact a generalized statement for the PGC, namely, that all PPAs have universal rights to their freedom and well-being.

7. For convenience, we speak of a single information provider as being involved at each of these stages. But of course, the developer and the transmitter of information can be (and often are) distinct from each other, and it is often collectives, rather than individuals, who are involved in these processes.

8. We reiterate that we are speaking here of what is morally (im)permissible, not of legality. So even if an invasion of privacy is not illegal, it may still be morally wrong.

9. This is likely to happen where there are not merely many channels of communication, but many sources of information. In many cases,

claims from a single source or a very restricted number of sources are transmitted by many different channels.

10. For a detailed discussion of the "unity of the right and the good" see Spence (2006, ch. 5; 2007). Virtues of character and their application to media practitioners as well as their impact on professional behavior will be discussed in more detail in Chapter 4.

References

Berlin, Isaiah (1958) *Two Concepts of Liberty*. Oxford: Clarendon Press.

Beyleveld, Deryck (1991) *The Dialectical Necessity of Morality: An Analysis and Defence of Alan Gewirth's Argument to the Principle of Generic Consistency*. Chicago: University of Chicago Press.

Brown, Debbie (2006) Refreshing twist in House race. *YourHub*, Feb. 15. http://denver.yourhub.com/Centennial/Stories/News/Politics Story~ 53039.aspx, accessed Nov. 2, 2010.

Dahl, Norman O. (1991) Justice and Aristotelian practical reason. *Philosophy and Phenomenological Research*, 51(1), 153–157.

David, Marian (2005) The correspondence theory of truth. In Edward N. Zalta (ed.), The Stanford Encyclopedia of Philosophy. http://plato.stanford.edu/archives/fall2005/entries/truth-correspondence/, accessed Nov. 8, 2010.

Deuze, Mark, and Yeshua, Daphna (2001) Online journalists face new ethical dilemmas: lessons from the Netherlands. *Journal of Mass Media Ethics*, 16(4), 273–292.

Drash, Wayne (2007) Internet cut in Myanmar, blogger presses on. *CNN*, Sept. 28. http://www.cnn.com/2007/WORLD/asiapcf/09/28/myanmar.dissidents/, accessed Nov. 2, 2010.

Dretske, Fred (1999) *Knowledge and the Flow of Information*. Stanford, CA: CSLI Publications.

Eco, Umberto (1989) *The Open Work*, trans. Anna Cancogni. Cambridge, MA: Harvard University Press.

Floridi, Luciano (2005) Is semantic information meaningful data? *Philosophy and Phenomenological Research*, 70(2).

Foster, Sophie (2007) Who let the blogs out: media and free speech in post-coup Fiji. *Pacific Journalism Review*, 13(2), 47–60.

Gahran, Amy (2005) Happy anniversary, Rathergate. *Poynter Online.* http://www.poynter.org/column.asp?id=31&aid=88712/, accessed Nov. 2, 2010.

Gewirth, A. (1978) *Reason and Morality.* Chicago: University of Chicago Press.

Gewirth, A. (1996) *The Community of Rights.* Chicago: University of Chicago Press.

Gewirth, A. (1998) *Self-Fulfilment.* Princeton: Princeton University Press.

Goldman, Alvin (2001). Social epistemology. In Edward N. ZaltaC (ed.), The Stanford Encyclopedia of Philosophy. http://plato.stanford .edu/entries/epistemology-social/, accessed Nov. 8, 2010.

Mason, Elinor (2006) Value pluralism. In Edward N. Zalta (ed.), The Stanford Encyclopedia of Philosophy. http://plato.stanford.edu/ archives/sum2006/entries/value-pluralism/, accessed Nov. 2, 2010.

McBride, Kelly (2006) The problem with citizen journalism. *Poynter Online.* http://www.poynter.org/column.asp?id=67&aid=97418, accessed Nov. 2, 2010.

Nussbaum, Martha (1986) *The Fragility of Goodness.* Cambridge: Cambridge University Press.

Pein, Corey (2005) Blog-gate. Columbia Journalism Review, Jan.–Feb. http://cjrarchives.org/issues/2005/1/pein-blog.asp, accessed Feb. 2, 2007.

Raz, Joseph (1999) *Engaging Reason: On the Theory of Value and Action.* Oxford: Oxford University Press.

Spence, E. H. (2006) *Ethics within Reason: A Neo-Gewirthian Approach.* Lanham, MD: Lexington.

Spence, E. H. (2007) What's right and good about Internet information? A universal model for evaluating the cultural quality of digital information. In Larry Hinman, Philip Brey, Luciano Floridi, Frances Grodzinsky, and Lucas Introna (eds), *Proceedings of CEPE 2007: The 7th International Conference of Computer Ethics: Philosophical Enquiry.* San Diego, CA: University of San Diego.

Spence, E. H. (2009a) The epistemology and ethics of Internet information. In Alessandro D'Atriand Domenico Sacca (eds), *Information Systems: People, Organizations, Institutions, and Technologies: ItAIS:The Italian Association for Information Systems.* Heidelberg: Physica, pp. 305–312.

Spence E. (2009b) The epistemology and ethics of media markets in the age of information. In Yvonne Thorhauerand Stefan Blachfellner (eds),

*Business Intelligence Meets Moral Intelligence,*International Review of Information Ethics (IRIE), 10 (Feb.), 45–52.

Spence E. H. (2009c) A universal model for the normative evaluation of internet information. *Ethics and Information Technology,* 11(4).

Spence, E. and Quinn, A. (2008) Information ethics as a guide for new media. *Journal of Mass Media Ethics: Exploring Questions of Media Morality,* 23(4), 264–279.

Stocker, Michael (1990) *Plural and Conflicting Values.* Oxford: Oxford University Press.

Walzer, Michael (1995) Are there limits to liberalism? *New York Review of Books,* Oct. 19, 28–31.

Williams, Bernard (1981) *Moral Luck.* Cambridge: Cambridge University Press.

Williams, Bernard (1985) *Ethics and the Limits of Philosophy.* Cambridge, MA: Harvard University Press.

Williams, Bernard (2002) *Truth and Truthfulness: An Essay in Genealogy.* Princeton: Princeton University Press.

Further reading

Boylan, M. (2000) *Basic Ethics.* Upper Saddle River, NJ: Prentice Hall.

Brey, P. (2007) Is information ethics culture-relative? *Journal of Technology and Human Interaction,* special issue "Information Ethics: Global Issues, Local Perspectives," 3(3), 12–24.

Ess, Charles (2006) An impending global ICE [information and computing ethics] age? East–West perspectives on information and computer ethics. Video presentation, North American Computing and Philosophy Conference, Aug. 10–12, 2006. NA-CAP 2006 @ RPI, Troy, NY, USA.

Floridi, Luciano (2002) What is the philosophy of information? *Metaphilosophy,* 33, 123–145.

Gorniak-Kocikowska, K. (1996) The computer revolution and the problem of global ethics. *Science and Engineering Ethics,* Apr.

Habermas, Jurgen. (1981) *Theorie des kommunikativen Handelns,* 2 vols. Frankfurt am Main: Suhrkamp. English translation *The Theory of Communicative Action,* trans. Thomas McCarthy. Cambridge: Polity, 1984–1987.

Johnson, Peter (2004) Rather's "Memogate": we told you so, conservatives say. *USA Today*, Sept. 26. http://www.usatoday.com/life/columnist/mediamix/2004-09-26-media-mix_x.htm, accessed Nov. 2, 2010.

Outing, Steve (2005) The 11 layers of citizen journalism. *Poynter Online*, June 15. http://www.poynter.org/content/content_view.asp?id=83126, accessed Nov. 2, 2010.

3

The Business of the Media and the Business of the Market

Introduction

Media organizations in modern societies are typically large commercial organizations, competing in a market. Moreover, the media itself plays an important role in the commercial life of modern society. But, as we point out in this chapter, the norms which govern market activities differ from, and can come into conflict with, the norms which govern the media. In this chapter we explore these norms, show the ways in which they may come into conflict, and argue that when they do, it is generally media norms which should prevail.

Media in the Marketplace

In liberal democratic societies such as the US, Great Britain, and Australia, the market is the central economic institution for the

Media, Markets, and Morals, First Edition. Edward H. Spence, Andrew Alexandra, Aaron Quinn, and Anne Dunn.
© 2011 Edward H. Spence, Andrew Alexandra, Aaron Quinn, and Anne Dunn.
Published 2011 by Blackwell Publishing Ltd.

production and distribution of goods and services. Producers compete with each other to provide what consumers want; in turn, consumers choose between a range of products. The market is a self-organizing process. Although it is not directed by any central authority it succeeds in providing a vast array of goods to consumers.

One of the striking features of the media in modern societies is the extent of its integration with the market. Most media is produced and distributed by (often very large) commercial organizations; we have on offer to us a huge variety of different kinds of media products, from TV game shows to movies, to gossip magazines, to specialist journals, to serious newspapers. The fate of these products is (to a large extent) determined by commercial considerations: those which appeal to public tastes survive; others perish.

Not only is much of the media produced by commercial organizations and made available to us like any other consumer good, but the media itself plays an important part in oiling the wheels of commerce. Mass media not only provides a forum in which producers can pay to advertise their wares to large audiences, but much of the content of that media consists in presentation and discussion of consumer goods and services. More broadly, the mainstream media plays an important role in setting the parameters of public discourse and opinion, not only in explicit discussion of matters of public policy and the like, but also in its presentation of images of "normal" life in sit-coms, soap operas, and so on. Undoubtedly, that presentation provides a very market-friendly view of the world.

Still, even if much of the media is run by business interests and subject to business pressures, the media (or at least central parts of it) surely cannot be seen as *just* another business. After all, the media is itself typically seen as one of the central institutions of modern society, on a par with the political system, organized religion, the education system, and indeed the market itself. The press (which must now be understood broadly, to include at least a central part of the media industry) is often referred to as "the fourth estate," meaning that it plays a role in the political system that is of

51

equal importance with that of the three official branches of government, the legislature, executive, and judiciary.[1]

More broadly, freedom of the press is often seen as a fundamental, and distinct, mark of a free society. The First Amendment to the US Constitution prohibits Congress making any law "abridging the freedom of speech or the press": the same amendment also prohibits Congress from making laws that restrict freedom of religion, assembly, and the right to petition government for redress of grievances. Although not every liberal democracy provides such constitutional protection, all accept the importance of a free press. A free press is vital to the life of a flourishing democracy in a number of ways. In the first instance it is a conduit for information about politics, economics, and public affairs. This allows members of a society to form informed views about these things; and it provides a bulwark against corrupt and oppressive behavior by the powerful, who are deterred by fear of exposure in the media. The media also provides a forum in which members of a society can express their various views to each other about such matters, and assert and explore their identity.

There is a tension, at least on the face of it, between the two ways of understanding the media implied by the above facts. On the one hand, much of the media consists of, or is controlled by, commercial organizations and is dominated by the logic of the market. On the other, the media has a role independent of, and even at times contrary to, narrow market interests.

Much of the discussion about the morality of the media in general and of media workers in particular reflects this tension. For example, proponents of a free press understand a free press to be simply one which cannot be restricted by the state. Just as anyone should be allowed to open a shop and stock it with whatever goods they want to, so anyone should be allowed to operate a media outlet and use it to express whatever views they wish (within the bounds of legality). On this approach, those who work in such outlets are in the same relationship to the owners of media organizations as shop assistants are to shop-owners. They are agents of the owners, whose function is to further the goals of the owners, provided this does not involve them in illegality or obvious immorality.

Others understand the free press, and consequently the role of those who work within it, in more substantive terms. They see the function of the free press as being defined by the dual goals of informing the public about matters of public interest, and of providing a forum in which the public can express and discuss its views. Correspondingly, the first duty of media workers such as reporters, photojournalists, and editors is to the realization of those goals. This means that they are not simply agents of the owners of the organizations for which they work, but should be granted some degree of independence and responsibility. Professionals such as doctors and engineers who work in large organizations nevertheless retain autonomy over much of their work, autonomy which may on occasion require them to act in ways which may not be in the short-term economic interests of such organizations. Similarly, it is claimed, media workers must retain autonomy over their work, even though the exercise of such autonomy may be contrary to the economic interests of the organizations for which they work or to the ideological stance of the owners of those organizations.

The market and the media are, then, at the same time closely intertwined in practice, and yet conceptually distinct. Any exploration of the role morality of those who work in the media, of the kind we undertake in this book, must consider the relationship between these two important institutions. This is our task in the rest of this chapter. First, we make some general remarks about the nature of fundamental institutions in pluralist societies. Then we consider the distinctive features of the institution of the market, on the one hand, and of the media on the other. Finally, we consider the implications the differences and relationships between these institutions have for the role morality of media workers.

Pluralism

Modern liberal democracies such as the USA, Australia, and the United Kingdom are pluralist societies. They are typically pluralist in at least a couple of ways. First, they contain a number of different ethnic and social groups, which may have quite different lifestyles and values. Second, they are composed of a range of relatively autonomous basic institutions such as the family, the political system, organized religion, the education system, the market, and so on; so understood, pluralist societies face two kinds of challenges: (1) The various ethnic and social groups which constitute pluralist societies must find a way of living together in a just and respectful way. (2) They must establish and promote the right kinds of relationships between the various basic institutions.

Here we focus on the issue of relationship between basic institutions. The first question we must address is: how do we identify and distinguish such institutions? Following the American philosopher Michael Walzer (1983), we suggest that each of the basic institutions constitutes a "sphere of justice," that is, a domain within which a distinctive good is (or should be) distributed according to principles of distributive justice which are specific to that domain. Consider the example of health care. The principle according to which such resources as hospital beds, medicine, and so on should be distributed is the need for health care. We would find it outrageous if a hospital bed were occupied by a healthy person at the expense of someone who is sick, for example. Or take the example of political power. In a democratic society, we believe that political power should be a function of popular support, as expressed in fair and open elections, rather than of, say, family lineage, as it was in aristocratic societies. In the case of the market, economic goods, including wealth itself, are distributed on the basis of the laws of supply and demand. Those who have goods which are in high demand and short supply – including their own labor power – are able to gain higher prices for them than those who possess goods in less demand.

Since each of the basic institutions has its own principle(s) of distribution, it follows that whether someone is entitled to goods in one institution, according to the principles of distribution specific to that institution, does not have any relevance to the question of whether they are entitled to goods in another. Possession of large amounts of money, for example, should not by itself allow a wealthy person to gain more political power than a poor person, since wealth is not a criterion for the distribution of political power. Conversely, possession of political power should not put someone in an advantageous position for gaining wealth, since political power is not an appropriate criterion for the distribution of market goods.

Notwithstanding, in many societies, pre-eminence in one particular sphere has often been translated into pre-eminence in a number of other spheres. In an aristocratic society, for example, the "well-born" gained not only social status, but also disproportionate political power, preferential access to education and desirable jobs, and so on. Similarly, in a theocratic society, religious leaders are favored. Walzer calls this phenomenon, where there is one sphere whose goods give access to the goods of other spheres, "dominance."

Over the past century or so, there have been two main forms of dominance. In socialist countries, such as the USSR and its satellite states, politics dominated other spheres, with political power translating more or less directly into wealth, prestige, preferential access to educational opportunities and other social goods for family members, and so on. In capitalist countries, on the other hand, it is the market which has tended towards dominance. Wealth has given those who possess it access to a range of other goods, especially political power – which in turn can be used to entrench the advantages of the wealthy. Many electoral innovations, such as public funding of political parties in proportion to their share of the vote, requirements for disclosure of political donations, restrictions on the amount of such donations to individual candidates, and so on can be understood as attempts to prevent, or at least limit, the translation of wealth into political power.

The answer to the question of whether market power is inappropriately dominating the workings of other basic institutions in modern societies is often complicated by the large degree of overlap between the market and those institutions. Above we mentioned health as an example of an institution whose defining good is distributed according to the principle of need. However, the institution of health care is deeply enmeshed in the market. Pharmaceutical companies, for example, are huge corporations, with turnovers in the billions, making immense profits. Similarly, skilled medical professionals such as surgeons charge high prices for their services, and earn large salaries.

But to say that health care is deeply involved with the market does not mean that it has simply become part of the market. Allowing market forces to operate in the area of health care may, as it happens, be the most effective way of producing and distributing many heath care goods. Pharmaceutical companies, for instance, have commercial incentives to produce better and cheaper medicines. But, on the approach being advocated here, as soon as the workings of the market do not allow for the distribution of health care goods according to the principle of need, it should be overridden or supplemented. For example, in many societies (for example, Australia and the UK) where much heath care is provided through market mechanisms, there is nevertheless a socially provided safety net, which guarantees that even those who lack the financial resources to buy their health care on the market can get the help they need when they are sick. Moreover, the behavior and self-understanding of many of those who are involved in the provision of health care can be understood only by reference to values that are internal to the sphere of health, rather than those of the market. For example, medical associations often forbid their members from using their medical expertise in a variety of ways which are held to be contrary to the goal of health, such as assisting in torture, even when such torture is legal and doctors are given substantial financial incentives for participation.

The Market and Its Norms

To understand the appropriate relationship between the market and the media we need to look more closely at the distinctive features of each. We begin with the market. For a market to exist there must be a number of interacting *market actors*, who are held to:

- come to market with pre-existing wants – to be fed, clothed, etc.;
- possess resources – money, goods, etc.;
- be rational, that is, act in a way that most effectively satisfies their wants;
- be self-interested, that is, not desire to satisfy the wants of others in the market;
- be independent, that is, no one can or will force another to give them what they want.

Given the existence of these features, the only way in which any market actor will be able to satisfy her wants is by means of trade – by mutual, voluntary exchange of goods. A market (for a good) occurs when there are market actors who are sellers and buyers; these are people who have reason to engage in trade with each other. Sellers always prefer to sell for more rather than less, and buyers always prefer to buy for less rather than more. A properly functioning market depends on the existence of a number of competing sellers, and a number of different buyers. Competition between sellers motivates them to find ways to offer more attractive (cheaper, more effective) goods to buyers, while competition between buyers for scarce goods tends to drive prices up to the point where sellers can make a profit.

Understood in this way, there are a number of attractive features of markets. First, they tend to be effective means for the production and distribution of economic goods. Producers are provided with incentives to produce goods which consumers want, and only those goods. The major modern alternative to markets has been so-called command economies, in which decisions about what gets produced and who gets the goods which are produced are made by centralized bureaucracies. The history of such economies in places such as the former Soviet Union showed them to be far inferior to markets in satisfying the desires of consumers.

Second, there are moral reasons to approve of markets. We should allow people to participate in market transactions out of respect for their autonomy. Above, we pointed out that market transactions take the form of trades, in which rational individuals freely choose to exchange goods with each other. Respect for autonomy requires that rational individuals be allowed to do what they want, provided that they do not hurt others in so doing. Since trades involve mutually agreeable behavior, it follows that there is a strong presumption that they should be respected.

We should also allow people to participate in market transactions because the world is likely to be a better place if they do so. Because both parties to a trade are, by hypothesis, rational, self-interested, and independent, they will enter into a trade only if they have good reason to believe that they will be more satisfied after it than before. Since a world in which there is a greater amount of satisfaction is in itself better than one in which there is less, a trade has the seemingly magical property of increasing the value in the world while leaving unchanged its material elements.

Market actors tend to internalize and act according to what we might call *market norms* – attitudes and modes of behavior that govern the production, circulation, and valuation of economic goods. Only in a group in which such norms are accepted are we likely to have a functioning market. The most important of these norms (based on Anderson 1993, 143–147) are:

- *impersonality* – the only features of individuals that matter are economic – social status is abolished in the market;
- *egoism* – individuals pursue their own interests, independent of consideration of the interests of others;
- *exclusivity* – purchase of a good gives exclusive access to its benefits;
- *want regardingness* – production responds to "effective demand," irrespective of reasons for that demand – this means, for example, that food producers should provide less nourishing but more palatable food, if that is what consumers want;

- *orientation to "exit" rather than "voice"* – if a consumer is unhappy, for whatever reason, with some commodity or transaction they will simply "exit" – go elsewhere in the market – rather than engage with the provider in attempt to get them to change their product or behavior (in other areas of our life, such as family relationships or political association, by contrast, we engage in dialogue to try to influence each other – we make use of our "voice").

The Media and Its Norms

Now let us consider the distinctive features of the media. Here our focus is on what we might think of as the "serious" media, concerned with what John Stuart Mill called "the business of life," such as morality, religion, politics, and social relations (Mill, 1999, ch. 2). It is a mark of such media that they claim to provide true information (as discussed in Chapter 2) about, and well-informed and reasoned discussion of, these issues. Of course, these activities of information and discussion are very much part of, and of fundamental importance to, our ordinary life. At least in part, then, the media functions as an extension and supplementation of activities which would occur anyway. Similarly, we need to look at the importance we attach to these activities to understand the role and status of the media.

Of particular importance to the role and self-understanding of the modern media is the doctrine of *freedom of the press*. This is often seen as an extension of the notion of free speech, applied to the activities of the press. Here we look at this notion of free speech, before considering its implications for the role of the press.

Any modern discussion of free speech must start from the influential defense of free speech by the nineteenth-century philosopher John Stuart Mill, especially as found in his work *On Liberty* (1999). For Mill, the value of free speech was itself derived from the more fundamental importance of freedom of thought. In turn, freedom of thought was to be valued because thought guides action. It is only if we have accurate, well-grounded, and properly informed beliefs that we are likely to be able to act in ways which will actually advance our interests. (As we saw in Chapter 2, moral theorists such as Alan Gewirth hold that we all have rights to freedom in virtue of our nature as purposive agents.) Freedom of speech is, according to Mill, "practically inseparable" from freedom of thought. It follows that, for Mill, freedom of thought does not simply mean being allowed to think what you want. It involves the freedom to strive towards a well-founded, internally consistent, and satisfying body of beliefs. Discussion is of fundamental importance in achieving such a body of beliefs. Having discussions with others is necessary to gain information, to develop critical capacities, and to clarify and critique one's own views. So freedom of speech means more than being able to say what you like. Indeed, freedom of speech, in the sense in which Mill used the term, is probably more accurately called freedom of discussion.

Mill presented two kinds of interrelated reasons in favor of free speech, so understood. First, he thought that it was more likely to allow the truth to emerge. Given our limited experience and intellectual capacity, and our tendencies to wishful thinking, self-delusion, and conformity, our beliefs are more likely to be reliable if they have been subject to a process of testing and contestation. As Mill puts it:

> Complete liberty of contradicting and disproving our opinion is the very condition which justifies us in assuming its truth for purposes of action ... The beliefs we have the most warrant for, have no safeguard to rest on, but a standing invitation to the whole world to prove them unfounded ... This is the amount of certainty attainable by a fallible being, and this is the sole way of obtaining it. (Mill 1999, ch. 2)

Second, the exercise of free speech is necessary for the development of our critical faculties, which help us to be able to discriminate between more and less justified claims to truth. A society of freely interacting, critically competent truth-seekers, in which a variety of different views are presented and vigorously contested, is one in which true beliefs are more likely to be generally held.

There are, then, two conditions for free speech, understood in something like Mill's sense (we here follow Lichtenberg 1987.) First, people must be protected against interference – they must have an effective and reliable right against being prevented from saying what they believe and testing their beliefs against others. In the first instance, then, the right to free speech is a so-called "negative right" – that is, a right against interference. It is important to note that even though *others* do not have a right to prevent us from doing what we want to in some area of our life, it does not follow that we should think we are permitted to do whatever we feel like doing. In the case of free speech, for example, others should not prevent us from speaking as we wish, but this does not mean that *we* should not feel any constraints on what we say – far from it. Arguably, we should not even engage in idle gossip about others, even if the subject matter of the gossip is not malicious, where doing so indicates a lack of respect for the people we are gossiping about.

While the assurance of non-interference is a necessary condition for free speech, it is not sufficient. Mill himself was a keen observer of the rise of "mass society" in the nineteenth century, with the rapid urbanization and homogenization of British society fostered by the forces of industrialization and economic development, including what we would now refer to as the mass media. Mill thought that these forces tended to push people towards a sameness of thought and behavior. Where such a deadening conformity occurs, non-interference by itself will not guarantee true freedom of speech.

The second condition for freedom of speech is the existence of a multiplicity of divergent but interacting voices. Where such voices do not arise spontaneously, or cannot be heard where they do arise, respect for freedom of speech may require more than simply not interfering with people's speech. In such a case, freedom of speech may also require actively intervening to ensure that a diversity of views is presented and seriously discussed – in, say, the education system, or if needs be, in the popular media. It *may* – whether it actually *does* is a matter for decision on a case-by-case basis.

From a Millian justification of free speech – as an indispensable means to the attainment of the truth – we can derive a justification of freedom of the press in a democratic society, which can be under-stood as free speech in a particular institutional setting. In a large and complex modern society, the press is of fundamental impor-tance as a means to allow us to gain information, to develop critical capacities, and to clarify and critique our own views about matters of social significance. As noted above, these provide the bases for the value of free speech, so any attempt to prevent the press from playing this role of providing information and discussion is an attack on the freedom of the press.

It is important to emphasize that the right to a free press (like other rights) imposes limits on what *others* may do to interfere with the choices made by the media (to publish or not, how information is presented, and so on). But from the fact that others (especially the government) should not forcibly constrain the press, it does not follow that the press should not constrain itself, or that it cannot be criticized for its actions. It is simply a mistake to think that because we have a right to do something, it is right for us to do it. So, just as the right to free speech does not mean that we cannot be criticized for anything we say, freedom of the press does not license the press to print anything it judges the reading public may find interesting. Freedom of the press no more justifies the retailing of salacious gossip about public figures, for instance, than freedom of speech justifies doing the same about our neighbors.

On the one hand, part of the role morality of the media is to provide information to people about things that are of interest to them and, it seems, there is a good deal of interest in the private lives of public figures. On the other hand, the persistent intrusion of the press into people's private lives, and the broadcasting of the (true and false) details of their personal affairs, clearly constrains their capacity to enjoy their rights to freedom and well-being, rights which are part of universal public morality. But since, as we argued in Chapter 2, universal public morality trumps role morality when the two conflict, the media is not justified in printing such gossip. Similarly, it is at least arguable that the newspapers which published the so-called "Muhammad cartoons," which portrayed the prophet Muhammad as a terrorist, were not justified in doing so: the cartoons gratuitously offended the religious sensibilities of a group which was already feeling marginalized and vulnerable, and predictably provoked militant responses. (This case is discussed further in Chapter 6.) The newspapers that published the cartoons can be criticized for gross disrespect of the beliefs of others, as well as irresponsibility. The response to criticism by appeal to freedom of the press is simply beside the point, since it was not generally being claimed that the newspapers had exceeded their legal rights, but rather that they should have used those rights more responsibly.

Just as freedom of speech implies a right of non-interference, so does freedom of the press. There is a strong presumption against the press being stopped from publishing what they wish. But just as non-interference is not the whole of freedom of speech, neither does it exhaust the meaning of freedom of the press. Again, freedom of the press also implies the presentation of a multiplicity of divergent but interacting voices.

As with freedom of speech in general, one important justification for valuing the representation of as wide a range as possible of different voices in the press is that this helps discover and promulgate the truth. But in a democratic, pluralist society there are also specifically political reasons for such representation. In a democracy, every person is supposed to be considered of equal value. While it is impossible for each individual to be given a forum for the expression of their views in the press, it is not so for each significant group – classes, ethnic groups, and so on. In being given such a voice the existence and value of such groups is, in effect, being affirmed both to their own members, and to society at large. Conversely, if the beliefs and attitudes of only some groups are represented in the mainstream press, the implicit message is that it is only these groups which really matter.

We are now in a position to outline the norms that do (ideally) guide the press. From our discussion of free speech it is clear that the fundamental norms are those of:

- *Truth-valuing*. The press should try to discover the truth, and present it in an accessible form. (The general justification for this is given in Chapter 2 – insofar as truth is a necessary condition of information, the media are committed to the norms of truth-valuing and truthfulness.)

- *Objectivity.* The press should be objective in its presentation of material. Objectivity includes but is wider than truth-seeking. For in matters of opinion, such as views about the merits of different political ideologies or moral stances, it is arguable that there is no straightforward fact of the matter. Nevertheless, the discussion of such views should still be objective, in that they are presented as fully and fairly as possible.
- *Representativeness.* The press should be representative, both of the range of views held in a society, and of the existence of the various social groups which constitute that society.

These norms are fundamental in that it is by reference to them that we develop and apply more fine-grained guidelines about media ethics. For instance, it is by reference to the norm of truth-valuing that we decide whether, and how, photojournalists are entitled to manipulate images. The norm of representativeness may be useful in deciding whose views a journalist should seek out in the course of researching a story about, say, the impact of illegal immigration, in judging the performance of a newspaper over a period of time, in evaluating the merits of proposed legislation to prevent cross-media ownership, and so on.

Of course, this is not to say that the press always acts in conformity with these norms, or even always aims to. No doubt journalists often write stories which are simply paraphrases of press releases, with no attempt to ascertain their veracity or to canvass a range of views. And, clearly, media proprietors often use their position to promote their own interests, or those of their class or favored political group (detailed examples of this are given in Chapters 5 and 6). But to call these norms ideals is not to identify them as simply pious wishes, which bear only an accidental relationship to the behavior of the media, and to the responses such behavior generally provoke. Rather they underlie the media's self-understanding and our attitudes to the media. Think what happens, for example, when credible claims are made that an important report in a reputable news outlet has been based on fabricated materials or radically incomplete information. There will be public concern, even anger: the news organization will try to show that the claims are false or, if they are proven to be true, respond with apologies, disciplinary action against offending journalists, actions to prevent a repetition, and so on.

A famous case which demonstrated the workings of these norms and exemplified the nature and importance of the freedom of the press was that of the Pentagon Papers.

The Pentagon Papers

In 1967, against the background of increasingly bitter domestic opposition to the Vietnam War, US Secretary of Defense Robert S. McNamara commissioned the Department of Defense to prepare a history of the United States' politico-military involvement in the war. The huge (47-volume, 7,000-page) secret report made it clear that the American people had been deceived by their leaders at every step: about the reasons for US escalation, about the way in which the war was being fought, and about the prospects for success. One of the authors of the report was Daniel Ellsberg, a brilliant scholar and former Marine. Ellsberg had been a committed supporter of US involvement, but had slowly become convinced that the war was unwinnable, and that the US people had to be told the truth about a war in which almost 60,000 of their soldiers were eventually to die. Dismayed by the refusal of his political masters to even contemplate the option of a US withdrawal, and frustrated by the unwillingness of anti-war politicians, to whom he had given sections of the report, to make their contents known, Ellsberg decided that he had no option but to use the press.

Ellsberg provided a full set of what became known as "The Pentagon Papers" to *New York Times* reporter Neal Sheehan. The *Times* published excerpts on June 13, 1971, with the promise of

65

more to come. On June 15, the US government obtained a temporary court injunction that stopped the *Times* from publishing more of the papers. Ellsberg made copies of the papers available to others newspapers, and on June 18, the *Washington Post* began publishing excerpts. The *Post* was enjoined. Excerpts then began appearing in the *Boston Globe*, the *Chicago Sun-Times*, the *St. Louis Post-Dispatch*, and so on. Eventually, excerpts were published in 17 newspapers.

Meanwhile, legal maneuvers continued, leading inexorably to the Supreme Court. The US government argued for continuation of the injunction, claiming that publication would cause "irreparable injury to the defense interests of the United States." A majority of the Court ruled against the government. Importantly, they did not deny the government's claim that publication would harm the national interest. Justice White, for example, wrote that:

> I do not say that in no circumstances would the First Amendment permit an injunction against publishing information about government plans or operations. Nor, after examining the materials the Government characterizes as the most sensitive and destructive, can I deny that revelation of these documents will do substantial harm to public interests. Indeed, I am confident that their disclosure will have that result.

Similarly, Justice Stewart stated that:

> We are asked, quite simply, to prevent the publication by two newspapers of material that the Executive Branch insists should not, in the national interest, be published. I am convinced that the Executive is correct with respect to some of the documents involved.

Nevertheless, they held that since publication would not result in "direct, immediate, and irreparable harm" (as, say, publishing the sailing schedule of a troopship in a time of war might), the presumption in favor of allowing the press freedom to decide what to publish must prevail. Stewart reaffirmed the role of a free press in the life of a democracy and its special importance in matters of national defense:

> In the absence of the governmental checks and balances present in other areas of our national life, the only effective restraint upon

executive policy and power in the areas of national defense and international affairs may lie in an enlightened citizenry – in an informed and critical public opinion which alone can here protect the values of democratic government.

The motivation of the newspapers in publishing the Pentagon Papers was clearly to give the American public information on a matter of vital concern, information which would have been withheld from them if it were not for the action of the newspapers. They went ahead and published in the face of government opposition and threats of legal action, and despite the fact that doing so would predictably upset significant sectors of their readership. The publication of the Pentagon Papers had a lasting impact on the national debate over the war in Vietnam. It stands as a clear example of the press acting in accordance with what we have identified as the fundamental norms of the media, and of the value of a free press.

The Media and the Market

We have pointed out that much of the media is, as business, governed by market norms, and at the same time, governed by its own (media) norms. We are now in a position to understand more clearly where the points of tension arise between these two sets of norms, and so better placed to see whether, and how, such tensions can be resolved.

First, we should note that there is in principle no reason why the media cannot act in accordance with the media norms outlined above, and at the same time be a thriving business enterprise. Indeed, if we compare the record of media organizations in the Western world, most of which have been run as businesses, with that of their counterparts in former communist states, which were an arm of the state, there is no question that the Western media did far better in behaving according to media norms. This is not surprising. In a healthy democratic society, there is a demand for reliable information and access to a range of opinions, which media organizations compete to provide.

That said, the reality of course is that often the media, driven by business considerations, do not act according to media norms. Moreover, the trend towards greater concentration of media ownership, and the assimilation of serious media organizations into giant vertically integrated corporations, generate concerns that the media is more likely to be driven purely by commercial considerations, even when these conflict with media norms.

Let us consider some of the ways in which the norms of the market and those of the media can come into conflict. First, whereas a business is legitimately motivated only by what is in its own interests ("egoism"), the media must be motivated by concern for the public interest, since each of the media norms has a base in public interest. Second, and relatedly, businesses should aim to provide only what customers want ("want-regardingness"), since it is by so doing that that they will most effectively achieve what is in their (commercial) interests. The media, on the other hand, may have duties such as to report certain facts, or to allow particular points of view to be put, because it is in the public interest that such things are aired, even if most of their consumers would prefer not to be confronted by those facts or points of view. Third, market norms are oriented to "exit" rather than "voice" – if a potential transaction is perceived by one of the parties not to be in their best interests (because for example, they can get a better deal elsewhere), then they have no obligation to the other party to continue to deal with them. On the other hand, since one of the basic functions of the media is to provide a forum for the expression of diverse views, media norms are oriented to "voice" rather than "exit."

There is a strong presumption that media norms should prevail when they conflict with market norms. (As we explain in more detail below, this presumption may be defeasible on those rare occasions when the very survival of a media organization depends on giving priority to a market norm.) The rationale for this can be explained in terms of means and ends. First, let us make some observations about the nature of means and ends. There are some things or activities that we value *only* as a means to a distinct end. So we engage in housework as a means to having a clean house (our end or goal). There are some things which we value not simply as means to ends, but also as ends in themselves. We may eat both because it is something we enjoy doing (it is an end in itself) and because we believe we need to be nourished (and eating is a means to this end). Finally, we may value some things as ultimate or final ends, that is, things which we value in themselves and which serve no further purpose. One of the marks of rational activity is that there are the right kinds of relationships between our various ends and the means we use to achieve them – for example, that we use means which are actually likely to allow us to achieve our goals.

Now let us consider the different kinds of norms that may apply to standard commercial organizations as against those that apply to media organizations. Consider, first, a standard business such as a carpet manufacturer. Clearly, the carpet manufacturer will have as one of its ends the making of carpets that are attractive to potential customers. Thus, the manager might decide to introduce a new range of carpets. The introduction of the new range is a means to producing carpets that are attractive to potential customers. However, the end of producing carpets that are attractive to potential customers is itself a means to a further end, that is, to make profits. Making profits is in fact the ultimate end of the business: it is by reference to this end that decisions about what it does should be made.

Now consider a media organization. Again, one of the ends of the media organization is to make a profit. Accordingly, many of the decisions that the organization takes, such as changing the layout of a newspaper to make it more eye-catching, or hiring a popular columnist, will be explained as means to that end. But unlike the carpet manufacturer, the making of a profit is not the ultimate end of the organization. Rather, the discovery and transmission of information and the provision of a forum for the expression of opinions are the ultimate ends of the organization. Since the end of making a profit is subordinate to (i.e., is itself a means to) these ends, when there is a conflict between acting in a way that will

gain more profit and achieving the ultimate ends of the organization, the organization should not act in the way that will lead to the
gaining of more profit. In other words, when market norms
and media norms come into conflict, it is the media norms which
should prevail.

At least, this is generally true. However, matters are complicated
by the fact that making a profit is not simply a means to achieving
the ultimate goals of a media organization, but a *necessary* means to
its achievement. Where media organizations are businesses, they
cannot survive without remaining commercially viable. And if they
do not survive, they cannot fulfill their function as media organizations. So it is perfectly legitimate, indeed desirable, for media
organizations to take commercial considerations into account in
decision-making. It may even be that on particular occasions there
should be compromises between business and media norms. For
example, a newspaper is perhaps justified in pandering, at least up
to a point, to the public's appetite for celebrity gossip, in order to
boost its circulation and advertising revenue, and in providing less
hard news where this is necessary to allow it to survive, or to have
sufficient resources to go on collecting news at all. It may be justified
in so doing, but if it is, the justification cannot simply be that
it helped make profit – it must be that the newspaper would
be unduly handicapped in its media role if that profit were
not generated.

The argument we have been making here about the relationship
between market and media norms depends of course on the truth of
the claim that the media organizations are more than simply
businesses. And that claim might be denied – and sometimes
(apparently) is. But if media organizations *are* simply businesses
it is hard to see what force claims about the freedom of the press can
have. Why should the press be treated any differently from any
other business if in fact that is all it is? Whenever a media proprietor
or editor resists government interference or regulation in its workings by appeal to the freedom of the press, they are, at least
implicitly, acknowledging that the media is an institution in its
own right, not just a part of the market.

Conclusion

In this chapter we have looked at the relationship between two of the major institutions of modern societies – the media and the market – which differ in function and guiding norms. As a matter of fact, the two institutions are intertwined, with the media deeply involved in the market in a variety of ways: the media support and facilitate the market; much of the media are, or are controlled by, commercial organizations. This creates the potential for the norms of the market to come into conflict with media norms within media organizations – should the truth be published, for instance, if doing so is likely to alienate readers and advertisers? As we have pointed out, the two sets of norms are not intrinsically incompatible: there is a market for accurate information and diverse opinion. However, as a matter of fact they often do come into conflict. The question then becomes which should prevail. The burden of our argument in this chapter has been that we find the answer to that question by coming to a proper understanding of the notions of free speech and the freedom of the press. Free speech is fundamental to the development of autonomous individuals and to a functioning democratic society. As such, it must be protected and fostered by any decent society. The media plays an essential role in the "speech" of large, complex societies of the kind we live in, so "freedom of the press" is a particular expression of the broader notion of free speech. Freedom of the press protects the media from interference by governments or other powerful bodies, but it also obliges the media itself to act in ways which are consistent with the underlying rationale for that freedom. In particular, it obliges them to be guided by what we have identified as media norms, even when doing so may not maximize profits.

Chapter study questions

1. Do you think that the media industry should be less subject to government control and regulation than other industries? If so, why?

71

2. Outline two arguments for freedom of speech which also support freedom of the press.
3. Would Mill think that the mere fact that the press is not subject to censorship and is (mostly) controlled by private interests mean that it is truly free? If not, what else would be required? Do you agree?
4. In his judgment in the Pentagon Papers case, Justice White accepted that publication of the papers could harm public interest. Nevertheless, he did not support banning their publication. Why not? What do you think?
5. "A shop-owner can tell their staff what goods to stock. Similarly, a newspaper proprietor is entitled to tell his or her editorial staff what line to run and what news to report." Is the proprietor so entitled?

Note

1. While this is the sense now typically given for the term, when "fourth estate" was first used to refer to the press, in eighteenth-century France, the three other "estates" were the nobles, clergy, and commoners.

References

Anderson, Elizabeth (1993) *Value in Ethics and Economics*. Cambridge, MA: Harvard University Press.

Lichtenberg, Judith (1987) Foundations and limits of freedom of the press. *Philosophy and Public Affairs*, 16(4), 329–355.

Mill, John Stuart (1999) *On Liberty*.Peterborough: Broadview. (Originally published 1859.).

Walzer, Michael (1983). *Spheres of Justice*. New York: Basic Books.

Further reading

Rudenstine, David (1996) *The Day the Presses Stopped: A History of the Pentagon Papers Case*. Berkeley: University of California Press.

4

Professionalism in Behavior and Identity

Introduction

At the heart of this chapter is an argument that the development of ethical ways of behaving can (but not inevitably *will*) be strengthened by identification with the idea of professionalism. So the chapter begins with an exploration of definitions of professionalism, emphasizing the centrality of both autonomous action and the concept of service. It then looks at how journalists in particular have interpreted and applied ideas of professionalism to their work. There is no single set of agreed criteria for defining a profession, and there are particular problems in relation to the practice of journalism. While journalists in some countries such as the United States of America may prefer to think of themselves as practicing a profession, others actively resist such a label, preferring to argue they are exercising a craft or trade. Many British and Australian journalists think like this, even as journalism educators may be

Media, Markets, and Morals, First Edition. Edward H. Spence, Andrew Alexandra, Aaron Quinn, and Anne Dunn.

trying to "professionalize" the preparation of young journalists. The American philosopher and educator James Carey (1980) long ago warned of dangers in professionalizing journalism, while Barbie Zelizer (1993) has suggested the frame of professionalism may be too limited.

Having set a framework for professionalism, the chapter then explores this in practice – that is, through ways journalists and public relations practitioners have behaved and how they have identified themselves as professionals – using case studies from Britain, the USA, and Australia. They begin with one that shook to its core one of the most prestigious media organizations in the world, the BBC, and called into question the universal television practice of editing. As a result of the case of the Queen and Annie Leibovitz, not only the BBC but also other media organizations began to question such ubiquitous "professional" practices as the "reverse" shot, and how they are applied. The second case study considers the assumption that a journalist must always protect his or her sources if revealing them would cause them harm; as we shall see, this ethical code can be used in ways that raise more complex ethical questions.

The final section of the chapter, "New Media, New Challenges," explores the implications for professional identity and ethical practice of the new media. The term "new media" is used to include digital non-linear media and its distribution on the Internet and mobile devices. The new media profoundly affects not only the day-to-day work of journalists, but also the relationship between media producers and media audiences. A case study considers the effects and implications of these new conditions.

Professionalism

Defining "professionalism" is notoriously difficult and the definitions are seldom disinterested, as those who wish to be identified as professionals advocate their own position, for a range of reasons (Reese 2001, 175). In relation to journalism this is partly historical and reflects the changing nature of journalistic work as well as changing definitions of journalism itself. Reese and Cohen argue that journalism "is quite different from the traditional learned professions such as medicine," on the grounds that medicine imposes barriers to entry and offers a "significant judgemental autonomy for the practitioner," while journalism does neither (Reese and Cohen 2000, 217). On the other hand, Dickinson argues that when journalists protest against perceived threats to their "journalistic independence," this can be seen as "expressions of the claim to professional autonomy" (Dickinson 2007, 203). Hartley has argued that journalists' lack of control over their conditions of work precludes journalism from developing as a profession at all; it is a trade (Hartley 1996, 35). He describes it as "wobbl[ing] in status" between "proletarian" and "professionalization." And what he uses to distinguish professionalization is "codes of ethics, disciplinary procedures" (Hartley 1996, 36). If codes of ethics and disciplinary procedures are the marks of a profession, then it could be argued that public relations (PR) bears those marks more visibly than journalism does. In Australia, the USA, and the United Kingdom, as in many other countries, journalism, PR, and advertising industry bodies all have codes of ethics. But in Australia, for example, the only code with a requirement that its members report breaches of it is that of the professional association of the public relations industry, the Public Relations Institute of Australia (PRIA). Hartley's complaint is thus that Australian journalists have no power to discipline those who breach the code of ethics, unlike doctors or lawyers, and that journalism cannot therefore be called a profession.

Sociological accounts of professionalism offer two approaches: *power* and *traits* (Tumber and Prentoulis 2005). *Power* approaches emphasize professional recognition as a means of achieving prestige and various forms of influence, for example managerial, social, and political influence, while *traits* approaches require either a single trait or a set of traits to be present before an occupation is considered a profession. These can range from income level, to formal education, to licensing and self-regulation, among other possibilities. Journalism may enjoy influence, and public relations cannot prosper without it, but journalists and public relations practitioners, as occupational groups, do not enjoy much prestige in the eyes of the general public. In successive surveys, both rate about the same or lower in public trust as used-car salesmen. Neither line of work is particularly well paid, especially journalism, nor are there any formal educational requirements to work in either role. On the power dimension then, neither journalism nor public relations would seem to qualify for recognition as professions.

Turning to the traits approach, there is somewhat more of an argument to be made. Prasad and Prasad (1994, 1438) argue that each occupational group calling itself a profession does so on the basis of "an influential set of beliefs which define the nature of professionalism and legitimate the `professions´ within society." Typically, a definition of professionalism will equate it with "credentialed expertise, with disinterested service, and with a strong adherence to a set of occupational norms" (Prasad and Prasad 1994: 1438). Further, professionalism may be said to involve "developing competence through education or experience and ensuring full, ethical application of that competence" (Pollard and Johansen 1998, 357). In Australia, the UK, and the United States journalists are not admitted to the occupation of journalist on the basis of "credentialed expertise." Only about half of all recruits to journalism cadetships in Australia, for example, have media, communication, or journalism degrees (although today they will probably have at least a bachelor's degree), and there is as yet no system of industry accreditation for these degrees as there is in the UK and USA. Even where there is such industry recognition, research suggests that recruitment does not privilege accredited courses (see Dickson and Brandon 2000; Purdey 2000; Alysen 2001). Professionalism among media workers is thus more likely to be a matter of personal orientation and emphasis in the workplace than of a professionalized occupational structure. One such definition is that it brings "to bear on the task in hand a number of known and tried skills that will produce predictable results" (Hood 1987). But this is a very specific sense of "professionalism," and not one that necessarily reflects what it means to be a member of a "profession." Using Hood's definition, plumbers may be highly professional in their approach to their work, and similarly camera operators or electricians in a TV studio, but we do not normally call any of these occupations "professions."

Another complication arises from recent global economic changes that have seen media organizations merge with other, sometimes non-media, organizations, creating fewer, bigger corporations for which journalism is not the only or even the core business. When most journalists find work in such transnational organizations, the challenge they face becomes to negotiate between organizational goals and individual professional norms. Reese (2001) points to the effect at the "extra-media level." That is, as news organizations have increasingly been merged with other, not necessarily media, conglomerates, they invoke "some vision of professionalism" in order to protect and legitimate their own interests. The interests of the corporation are not always identical with the interests and purposes of the individual professional journalist. This has implications not only for the practice of journalism in the workplace but also for the way universities prepare journalists to enter the workplace. In the United States and to a lesser extent in the UK and Australia – so far – the corporate sectors, including media, "have sought through their philanthropy, subsidies and other institutional ties to affect how universities define and pursue being `professional'" (Reese 2001, 184). These changes to the political economy of the media and of universities suggest that it is more important than ever for those who work in the fields of media and communication to have a clear ethical understanding of the concepts of responsibility and obligation. The concluding chapter of this book considers the ideas of role models and moral excellence in the media.

Where sociologists might speak of "a professionalized occupational structure" or "occupational norms," in defining a profession, philosophers and others may consider what functions or goals a profession ought to serve, and their related principles or values. Thus, a definition of profession may be "a calling founded on a body of knowledge, a call to public service and an ethical framework for practice" (Beam 1990, cited in Reese and Cohen 2000, 217), or that it is an occupation that serves a moral ideal (Davis 2004).

One way of conceiving this moral ideal in terms of a professional framework is to borrow from a theory of ethics whose goal is based on an ideal and is frequently role-oriented. Virtue ethics, whose ideal is moral excellence, is a theory that is frequently used to form a role morality, so that participants in, for example, institutional roles will have a regulative ideal that guides their behavior. To better understand this professional framework it is first imperative to grasp the fundamentals of virtue theory.

Virtue Ethics and Professionalism

The roots of virtue ethics lie in ancient philosophy, most notably Plato and Aristotle, but also perhaps in much older ancient Chinese philosophy (Hursthouse 2003). What figures into virtue ethics is "motives and moral character, moral education, moral wisdom or discernment, friendship and family relationships, a deep conception of happiness, the role of emotions in our moral life, and the fundamentally important questions of what sort of person I should be and how we should live" (Hursthouse 2003). There are three fundamental concepts derived from classical Greek notions of virtue ethics that are central to understanding virtue theory; these are *virtue, phronesis,* and *eudaimonia.*

Virtue

Take, for example, virtue in regard to truthfulness. The virtuous person is not merely committed to *telling the truth.* Possessing the *virtue of truthfulness* implies that understanding what is good about truth is a deeply ingrained part of one's character, well entrenched in one's psyche. It does not depend only on the act of truth-telling but largely on what motivates someone to tell the truth and what he or she intends to achieve by being truthful.

Consider the case of Australian journalist Chris Masters, who employed covert methods for uncovering police corruption in the Australian state of Queensland (see also Chapter 9). Masters used hidden cameras and hidden audio recorders to document various sources and subjects that provided evidence that Queensland police were working for underworld crime syndicates. In some cases, police were said to have committed crimes as severe as contract murders. Thus, it seems that without using deceptive newsgathering methods, he would not have had the necessary evidence to uncover a severe case of police corruption (Masters 2004).

As is the case at times for the police and various other forms of military and law enforcement, lying used as a tool to meet the end of justice is sometimes paramount to truth-telling. By and large, it is justice that permits certain role players to omit truths or to deceive when it brings about the appropriate good.

Justice as journalistic virtue

Much as Aristotle regarded justice as the complete moral virtue, so too justice ought to be a governing agent-neutral virtue for journalists. Agent-neutral, in this context, means a virtue that calls for equal application to all persons, with no special consideration for an individual or discrete group. Plato and Aristotle understood justice as a virtue that penetrates more or less all matters of morality, one that includes notions of social justice and particular justice. Justice in this sense promotes the idea that persons, entities, or things generally ought to be handled according to how they *deserve* to be treated (Dahl 1991). Thus, a person ought to be treated in accordance with what they deserve based on some system (or systems) of merit; for example law-abiding citizens deserve the full rights of citizenship qua law because they have earned that right in being lawful.

Phronesis

Being virtuous involves what has been described as deeply ingrained, internal characteristics of persons, yet we have not determined what allows for such deep traits. How does a journalist *know* when something like a lie is permissible or impermissible in the role of the journalist? To answer this, we must explore the second central concept in virtue ethics, *phronesis*, or practical wisdom. Though practical wisdom is the focus of much scholarly debate, it is most simply understood as possessing the requisite knowledge to act according to virtue. Thus, being virtuous is in part dependent upon one's moral knowledge – *phronesis* or practical wisdom. Just as being a good doctor is dependent upon having knowledge about how to heal the sick, so being a virtuous person requires having intimate knowledge of what is good, not just abstractly, but through training and experience in a given role.

Good doctors know how to heal the sick because good doctors are appropriately educated, have the requisite experience, *and* are properly motivated to act on that knowledge in the right way. That said, the virtuous doctor, like any virtuous person, is often dependent upon certain favorable life conditions – a good family upbringing, and a moral and prudential education, wherein one hones the right dispositions and motives often in the early stages of one's *professional* moral development. Accordingly, practically wise persons (those with *phronesis*) have the "capacity to recognize some features of a situation as more important than others, or indeed, in that situation, as the only relevant ones" (Hursthouse 2003). However, to pursue moral knowledge – or to impart it to others – one must first have a conception of the good.

Eudaimonia

This leaves us with the third concept central to virtue ethics, *eudaimonia*, which is described by Aristotle as human flourishing. Aristotle's conception of *eudaimonia* (see also Chapter 2) is thought to be the "final end" or that at which all human activities are aimed – its ideal state involves living the best possible human life, and is the ultimate conception of the good. It is the beginning in terms of it being the impetus for being virtuous; it is the end insofar as living well or human flourishing is the result of a life lived by virtue. This connects with the previous two central concepts of virtue ethics: first, achieving some degree of *virtue* is crucial to developing good character, which, of course, is dependent upon one having *phronesis*, or moral knowledge, to pair with a good disposition – having the right intentions and motivations for one's actions. And the fundamental conception of the good is *eudaimonia*, or human flourishing, which is brought about by acting in accordance with virtue.

Taking virtue as a guide to being a journalism professional, we must consider what goals and virtues characterize professionalism in journalism, and (why and how) professionalism would make for better journalism. The following case studies are a starting point for discussion about two key virtues of media practitioners: truthfulness and accuracy. They will also address a fundamental issue in journalism regarding the use and limits to protecting the confidentiality of sources.

Truthfulness

The Editor, the Photographer and the Queen

In a smart London hotel early in July 2007, the controller of BBC1 was screening previews of the channel's new season of television programs to a small audience of entertainment journalists. Among the programs was a "fly-on-the-wall" documentary series about Queen Elizabeth II of England, *A Year with the Queen*. The controller, an experienced media manager called Peter Fincham, was reported as telling journalists that he was excited about the series, and mentioned in particular a moment during a photographic session of the Queen by American celebrity photographer Annie Leibovitz: "Annie Leibovitz gets it slightly wrong and the Queen walks out in a huff" (Holmwood 2007b). The journalists saw a trailer from the series that appeared to show Leibovitz asking the Queen to remove her tiara as it was "too dressy," and the Queen apparently responding (referring to the full robe of state she is wearing for the shoot), "Less dressy? What do you think this is?" In the next shot, the Queen has apparently abruptly left the room, as she is seen walking rapidly along, saying to a footman, "I'm not changing anything. I've done enough dressing like this, thank you very much." The problem was that the sequence of shots had been edited out of the order in which they had been recorded. The shot of the Queen walking and talking was taken *before* she arrived in the room in which she was to be photographed. By editing the sequence so this shot came *after* the Queen's exchange with Leibovitz, the program's producers make it appear that the exchange had caused the walk-out. Audiences have learned to read the visual language of film in a way that makes causal connections between consecutive shots. To edit the sequence in that way was thus deceptive; it made it appear that something had happened that had not in fact happened. In effect, the result was a lie.

The significance of this story for this book is in its aftermath. Not only did two people lose their jobs – the controller of BBC1 and the creative director of RDF Media, the company which had produced the program – but the ethics of routine professional practice were also called into question. It became apparent that many producers felt under increasing pressure in a rampantly competitive television industry to use editing techniques to heighten audience interest in ways that did not necessarily produce an authentic representation of events and behavior. A succession of such deceptions was revealed, including faked sequences, distortions, and unacknowledged reconstructions of events. A former BBC producer turned senior academic, Alison Cahn, described the editing room as "a very dangerous and tempting place" where "it's very easy to see people just as material" (Smith and Thorpe 2007). The danger of seeing people "just as material" lies in treating them just as means to an end (the end being a program sold, a program that rates well), and thus feeling free to produce what Cahn called "a very skewed version of the world."

The success and growth of so-called "reality TV" has introduced documentary techniques to programs primarily intended as entertainment rather than to convey information. It is worth noting that the creative director of RDF Media, the independent production company that made *A Year with the Queen* for BBC1, was credited with inventing the "life swap" genre, with shows such as *Faking It* and *Wife Swap* (Smith and Thorpe 2007). This in turn has made producers of television news, current affairs, and documentary programs sensitive to the credibility of their work for viewers. Another professional practice that came under scrutiny as a result of this case is widely used in news and current affairs interviewing. This is the "reverse" shot, also sometimes called a "noddy" shot, which is a version of changing the sequence in which shooting actually took place, in this case in order to create the effect of there being more than one camera at a scene when only one was used. The "noddy" shot is of the interviewer or reporter apparently responding with a nod or change of facial expression to the words of the person being interviewed. However, these reaction shots are nearly always recorded *after* the whole interview has been shot on one camera with the shot held on the interviewee's face. The editor then drops in the "noddies" at appropriate places, mainly to hold viewer interest by varying the shot, but they inevitably also influence viewers' interpretations of what has been said. For example, if a certain comment from the interviewee is followed by a smile and a nod from the interviewer, viewers may feel differently than if the comment were to be followed by an expression of disapproval or indifference.

Within a month of the deceptive preview clip, the commercial UK television network, Channel Five, announced it would no longer use "noddies" or other staged shots in its news reports. In so doing, Channel Five was acknowledging that unexamined habitual professional behavior could result in deception. News editor David Kermode said the new approach "would help restore viewers' trust" (Holmwood 2007a). He pointed out that viewers today are familiar with how television is made. Digital media technology means that viewers themselves may be making and uploading video; it also makes a "dissolve" edit from one shot to another very simple. Such an edit is evident to the viewer – who therefore knows an edit has been made – but need not interrupt the flow of the piece and enables it to be cut to the available time. The key lessons which seem to have come out of this case study, for UK broadcasters at least, are (1) not to do things that risk deceiving viewers, and (2) to recognize that viewers are not as easy to deceive as perhaps they once were.

Confidentiality

Confidentiality is recognized by the traditional professions – doctors, lawyers, and clergy – as a professional duty. It is increasingly invoked by others including journalists as "the duty of professional secrecy," one that "serves in part to reinforce their claim to professional status" and in part to strengthen their capacity to serve the public (Bok 1989, 116). For journalists, the relationship they have with their sources – the people on whom they rely for stories – can be morally complex. The story of *New York Times* reporter Judith Miller illustrates this very well.

Judith Miller and the Anonymous Source

In 2005, Judith Miller left the *New York Times* in a cloud of controversy, after 28 years, during which she had authored four books and been awarded a Pulitzer Prize, American journalism's highest accolade. In a *Washington Post* profile, writer Lynne Duke (2005) reported that Miller was said by her admirers to cultivate sources "really assiduously," and by her critics to be "too close to her sources." She was reined in by her own paper for the zeal with which she had pursued the so-called weapons of mass destruction (WMD) in Iraq, while embedded with a US army unit tasked with finding WMD in 2003. Miller had relied on sources later found to be unreliable; her paper published an apology for the "poor" reports.

In July 2003, former US ambassador Joseph C. Wilson published an op-ed, or opinion piece, in the *New York Times*, criticizing the Bush administration for "twisting" intelligence in order to justify its actions in Iraq. A week later, conservative political commentator Robert Novak revealed that Wilson's wife, Valerie Plame, was a covert CIA agent. Wilson claimed that his wife's position in the CIA had been leaked to Novak in retribution for his Op-Ed piece. A federal investigation was launched into the leaking of Plame's identity. It emerged that Miller had met with a political source two days after the Wilson piece was published, and in 2005, she was subpoenaed to appear before a grand jury. However, she refused to testify and ended up spending 85 days in prison, rather than name the source who had mentioned Plame's identity to her. Miller said – although not everyone believed her – that she was defending the First Amendment rights of journalists, because she did not believe her source had sufficiently waived the confidentiality agreement between them. The source was later revealed to be Lewis "Scooter" Libby, the Vice President's Chief of Staff (who was found guilty in 2007 of perjury, having lied during the leak investigation). After Libby telephoned Miller, she agreed to testify and was released from prison; at one point it appeared she might be charged with criminal contempt, which carries a much longer sentence than civil contempt.

So, was Miller right to choose jail rather than betray a professional confidence, made to her as a journalist, even though she never wrote about it? By invoking the First Amendment, this is what she claimed to be doing; her critics suggested Miller "needed to resuscitate her professional image" (Duke 2005) after the discredited Iraq WMD reports. Nonetheless, professional journalists' associations spoke out in defense of Miller and against the threat of legal action forcing disclosure of sources. The international journalists' organization, the Committee to Protect Journalists (CPJ), described the federal court as "setting an unfortunate example for the rest of the world" (IFEX 2005) and Venezuelan president Hugo Chavez cited Miller's case when answering international critics of his country's media laws. A number of other press and broadcast media organizations also called on the US Congress to support a proposed federal "shield law" that would grant journalists "absolute privilege," so they could not be compelled by the courts to disclose any information about their sources. Such shield laws already exist in a number of states (but not in many other countries, including Australia and the UK). The Inter American Press Association (IAPA) argued that the lack of safeguards guaranteeing the confidentiality of journalists' sources weakens the media's ability to keep the public informed.

Miller's justification for keeping confidentiality was that she had given her word that she would honor what Bok calls "the bonds and promises that protect shared information." That is, once a promise of silence is made, this in itself creates an obligation and thus "alienates ... some portion of one's freedom of action" (Bok 1989, 120). A journalist must face not only the legal compulsion to disclose, but also – and more often – economic and competitive pressures to reveal secrets. The duty to preserve secrets that features in journalists' – and other media professionals' – codes of ethics arises both from the power of a promise and from the public benefit that is seen to result from confidentiality. Society gains from allowing people to seek help from journalists in confidence, despite the risks. This is the argument of professionalism.

New Media, New Challenges

There is evidence that journalists feel a strong sense of a collective occupational identity (Tumber and Palmer 2004; Gall 2005; Dickinson 2007). Digital media are presenting new challenges to this shared identification. One challenge is in the growing move for media organizations to require journalists to be multiskilled enough to work across media platforms. For example, the video journalist, who is reporter, camera operator, and producer in one, can be seen as threatening the coherence of professional identity of each one of the roles he or she performs; alternatively, a new professional identity is emerging. Both scholars and editorial managers in media organizations (Cottle 1999; Blair 2004; Dyke 2004; Dickinson 2007) have suggested that the development of 24-hour, cross-platform newsrooms puts a degree of pressure on journalists that may be a partial explanation, if not an excuse, for journalism that is inaccurate at best, unethical at worst. Director of BBC news and current affairs, Helen Boaden, acknowledged this when she told a *Guardian* newspaper journalist: "The danger with 24-hour news is that it becomes a rolling service of rumour and speculation" (Wells 2005, cited in Dickinson 2007, 203).

A second, equally threatening challenge to professional journalism is the rise of the non-affiliated, amateur journalist-writer-producer, particularly on the Internet, through blogs, social networking, and other interactive sites, such as YouTube. The ease of use and accessibility of the means to produce digital media in combination with the Internet have enabled rapid growth and spread in so-called "user-generated" or "user-created" content. Akin to the "citizen journalism" that predated the Internet, user-generated content presents challenges not only to the professional status of journalism but also to the relationship – indeed, the definitional distinction – between the journalist and the audience for journalism.

This phenomenon has provoked wide-ranging discussion around the question of how to define both journalist and professional in such a situation. Deuze (2005) has argued that journalism must overcome its "operational closure" and embrace contributions from "the people formerly known as the audience" (Rosen 2006).[1] Ugland and Henderson choose to distinguish between "public communicators," "second-level journalists," and "top-level journalists." They argue that "a simple journalist/nonjournalist dichotomy" is misleading when today "there are potentially as many definitions of journalist as there are consumers of journalism" (Ugland and Henderson 2007, 253). In their model, the *public communicators* include both occasional contributors to public information dissemination and "professionals in advertising, public relations, or other fields whose communications are not designed to report on important events occurring in society" (254). While public relations practitioners in particular might take exception to this description, it enables the authors then to make a further qualitative distinction within "journalism," between the "second-level" and the "top-level." While *second-level journalists* "are engaged in a . . . regular, systematic, and conspicuous dissemination of news . . . their contributions are made with some predictability and purpose; [and unlike the contributions of the public communicators] they are not simply incidental to some other goal" (254). Second-level journalists, in this account, act professionally insofar as they are focused on telling "the truth," but they may not be trained as journalists or have regular paid work as such. Only the *"top-level"* of journalist emphasizes the "broader social impact of journalism and the responsibilities of journalists to act as stewards of the public interest" (258). Professional journalists are "those who are judicious, empathetic and who act in concert with the welfare of their fellow citizens" (Ugland and Slattery 2006); and these are also the characteristics of the "top-level" journalist. In other words "real journalists" demonstrate an understanding of and commitment to *values*, defined as the distinction of the professional (Ugland and Slattery 2006).[2]

Web Diary

Margo Kingston's *Web Diary* was started in July 2000 by the Australian *Sydney Morning Herald* newspaper. Margo is a journalist of many years' experience in political journalism who, when her editor gave her *Web Diary*, felt "too busy to learn new stuff." Initially, she did not invite contributions but found she received them anyway, as "online media [is] collapsing barriers to entry."[3] Margo realized that the Web offered a new relationship between journalist and audience when she began to receive emails that began "Oh gee, this is unusual, being able to talk back to a journalist." For this very experienced professional journalist, it was a discovery that people want to "talk back to a journalist."

The history of her *Web Diary* suggests that, while she may not have felt threatened by this, her managers were. Margo had seen "a great divide between the media and people" when she'd covered the political campaign of the Australian independent conservative member of parliament from Queensland, Pauline Hanson (Kingston 1999). To her, the initial experience of *Web Diary* was "like the answer to the question I'd been asking since the Hanson campaign ... I cannot tell you how excited I was." By February 2001, seven months after the first column had appeared, Margo was asking her audience what questions they would like her to ask of the people she interviewed; she had begun to open up a space that people could shape.

If Margo was excited, she was also "scared." When people are invited to express what they know and what they think, the result does not always conform to the values of mainstream journalism.

> When people started ... it did create a space where people of extreme views, either side, plus people who weren't articulate, like ordinary people, would come in and that would create major dramas. Like, there would be stuff published on *Web Diary* that wouldn't be published in the paper because it would be considered racist. But it was put in a context, it was an individual voice saying, actually articulating, I'm not racist, this is what I think. And then you can imagine the rush of people wanting to come in saying I think you're racist. And then someone might complain that I'd published a racist thing. So you know it became quite controversial but it worked because I – even though I hadn't thought about the ethics stuff, I was really clear about my values.

Eventually, concerned about the ethics of engagement with and between her contributors, Margo developed a code of ethics for *Web Diary* participants. She also wrote a "charter" for *Web Diary*, which included her belief that:

> There is a vacuum of original, genuine, passionate and accessible debate on the great political, economic and social issues of our time in the mainstream media, despite the desire of thinking Australians in all age groups to read and participate in such debates.

It took on as part of its mission, the desire to "spark original thought and genuine engagement with important issues which affect us all." Margo describes *Web Diary* as a "fantastic case study of how citizen journalism might work," but "management couldn't accept it." The reason is the threat to authority and credibility represented when "anyone" can be the source, "anyone" can write the news, offer an opinion, editorialize. For a newspaper of record such as the *Sydney Morning Herald*, any threat to authority and credibility is potentially devastating; these are the reasons people turn to it and its web site. How then to retain those crucial qualities while offering participation as an option for the online audience? Margo's answer is "the ethics, the ethics, the ethics"; this involves not only the "code of ethics" but also the nature of the relationship between the online newspaper and its readers: "Put your complete process out there – and give people some ownership. Trust in the process."

Unfortunately, the newspaper's managers felt unable to do this; by 2005, Margo was in dispute with them over the extent to which *Web Diary* had been "taken over" by user-generated content, and eventually she left the paper.

There is no doubt that digital media challenge professional media ethics. As we have seen, there are ethical issues aplenty given the relative ease with which "the former audience" can now act as journalists. In addition, the digital environment enables alteration and manipulation of text and images that is almost undetectable (except at source code level). This is something that we consider further in Chapter 8.

Conclusion

This chapter has considered the relationship between journalism, concepts of professionalism, and ethical behavior. While there continues to be a range of ways to define "professional" and "professionalism," the key element settled upon in this chapter is that of service, as a moral goal, embodied in moral virtues internalized by journalists, that is, in the role morality of journalism. While, again, there is ongoing debate about whether or not journalism is or should be a profession, it is clear that many if not most journalists consider public service to be one of the key moral goals of journalism. Given this, the case studies demonstrate the importance of an ethical framework for practice in relation to key functions of journalism: to be truthful, be accurate, and take an ethical approach to sources. This chapter has dealt mainly with journalists; the next section of the book will look at how these principles apply in considering other media practitioners, in public relations and advertising. It will take a closer look at the new media and its challenges, and then at the concept of corruption in the media.

Chapter study questions

1. After reading this chapter, what is your response to the question of whether or not journalists may be considered professionals? What can be said for and against the idea?
2. What widely accepted professional practices in media work other than journalism, such as public relations and advertising, can you think if that might present ethical dilemmas?
3. Discuss how the idea of a role morality (see Chapter 2) is applicable to the roles of media professionals.
4. This chapter has emphasized the work of journalists; how do you think the virtues of justice and truthfulness might apply to the work of media practitioners in fields other than journalism (see Chapter 2)?
5. Debate the question of confidentiality in media work: to what extent is it a moral obligation to respect a confidence, in the face of legal or other pressures to break it? Does it make a difference what kind of pressure (legal, economic) is brought to bear? In your discussion, consider the role of social media, such as Twitter and Facebook, which blur the distinction between public and private information.
6. Do you see the rise of new kinds of social communication on the Web as threatening to professionalism? Or does it mean that voices hitherto denied the opportunity can now speak out in the public domain?

Notes

1. Rosen acknowledges the use of the phrase "the former audience" by Gillmor (2004).

2. Ugland and Slattery (2006) also define professional journalists as people of *character*. This is something we will return to in the final chapter, when we consider moral excellence in the media.
3. All quotes from Margo Kingston are from a personal interview with her conducted by Anne Dunn in July 2006.

References

Alysen, B. (2001) Tertiary journalism education: its value in cadet selection at metropolitan media. *Asia-Pacific Media Educator*, 10, 100–111.

Beam, R. (1990) Journalism professionalism as an organization-level concept. *Journalism and Mass Communication Monographs*, 121, 1–43.

Blair, J. (2004) *Burning Down My Master's House: My Life at the New York Times*. Beverly Hills, CA: New Millennium Press.

Bok, S. (1989) *Secrets: On the Ethics of Concealment and Revelation*. New York: Vintage Books.

Carey, J. (1980) The university tradition in journalism education. *Carlton Journalism Review*, 2(6), 3–7.

Cottle, S. with Ashton, M. (1999) From BBC newsroom to BBC newscentre: on changing technology and journalist practices. *Convergence*, 5(3), 22–43.

Dahl, Norman O. (1991) Justice and Aristotelian practical reason. *Philosophy and Phenomenological Research*, 51(1), 153–157.

Davis, M. (2004) One-sided obligations of journalism. *Journal of Mass Media Ethics*, 19(3–4), 207–222.

Deuze, M. (2005) Towards professional participatory storytelling in journalism and advertising. *First Monday*, June. http://www.firstmonday.org/issues/issue10_7/deuze/#author, accessed Jan. 5, 2008.

Dickinson, R. (2007) Accomplishing journalism: towards a revived sociology of a media occupation. *Cultural Sociology*, 2(1), 189–208.

Dickson, T., and Brandon, W. (2000) Media criticisms of US journalism education: unwarranted, contradictory. *Asia Pacific Media Educator*, 8, 42–58.

Duke, L. (2005) The reporter's last take: in an era of anonymous sources, Judy Miller is a cautionary tale of the times. *Washington Post*, Nov. 10.

Dyke, G. (2004) *Inside Story*. London: HarperPerennial.

Gall, G. (2005) Back from the brink or still on the margins? The National Union of Journalists in the provincial newspaper industry in Britain. *Journalism*, 6(4), 422–441.

Gillmor, D. (2004) *We the Media* Sebastopol, CA: O'Reilly Media.

Hartley, J. (1996) *Popular Reality: Journalism, Modernity, Popular Culture.* London: Arnold.

Holmwood, L. (2007a) Five News to ban staged shots. *Guardian, Media Guardian*, July 16.

Holmwood, L. (2007b) Out of order. *Guardian*, July 16.

Hood, S. (1987) *On Television*. London: Pluto Press.

Hursthouse, Rosalind (2003) Virtue ethics. In Edward N. Zalta (ed.), *The Stanford Encyclopedia of Philosophy.* http://plato.stanford.edu/archives/fall2003/entries/ethics-virtue/, accessed Nov. 5, 2010.

IFEX (2005) CPJ says U.S. court decisions on journalists' right to safeguard their sources send the wrong message to the world. *IFEX*, June 30. http://ifex.org/international/2005/07/01/capsule_report_cpj_says_u_s_court/, accessed Nov. 10, 2010.

Kingston, M. (1999) *Off the Rails: The Pauline Hanson Trip.* Sydney: Allen & Unwin.

Masters, Chris (2004). Corruption Inc. Broadcast on *Four Corners*, July 6. Transcript at http://www.abc.net.au/4corners/content/2004/s1143925.htm, accessed Nov. 5, 2010.

Pollard, G., and Johansen, P. (1998) Professionalism among Canadian radio announcers: the impact of organizational control and social attributes. *Journal of Broadcasting and Electronic Media*, summer, 356–370.

Prasad, P., and Prasad, A. (1994) The ideology of professionalism and work computerization: an institutionalist study of technological change. *Human Relations*, 47(12), 1433–1458.

Purdey, H. (2000) Radio journalism training and the future of radio news in the UK. *Journalism: Theory, Practice and Criticism*, 1(3), 329–352.

Reese, S. (2001) Understanding the global journalist: a hierarchy of influence approach. *Journalism Studies*, 2(2), 173–187.

Reese, S., and Cohen, J. (2000) Educating for journalism: the professionalism of scholarship. *Journalism Studies*, 1(2), 213–227.

Rosen, J. (2006) The people formerly known as the audience. Posted to *Pressthink* on June 27, 2006. http://journalism.nyu.edu/pubzone/weblogs/pressthink/2006/06/27/ppl_frmr.html, accessed January 5, 2008. Also available from http://www.huffingtonpost.com/

jay-rosen/the-people-formerly-known_b_24113.html, accessed Nov. 5, 2010.

Smith, D., and Thorpe, V. (2007) A question of trust. *Observer*, July 15, 18–19.

Tumber, H., and Palmer, J. (2004) *Media at War: The Iraq Crisis*. London: Sage.

Tumber, H., and Prentoulis, M. (2005) Journalism and the making of a profession. In H. de Burgh (ed.), *Making Journalists: Diverse Models, Global Issues*, London: Routledge, 58–74.

Ugland, E., and Henderson, J. (2007) Who is a journalist and why does it matter? Disentangling the legal and ethical arguments. *Journal of Mass Media Ethics*, 22(4), 241–261.

Ugland, E., and Slattery, K. (2006) Ethics: fewer "journalists," more "professionals." http://www.digitaljournalist.org/issue0601/ethics.html, accessed Jan. 5, 2008.

Wells, M. (2005) Have I got news for you. *Guardian*, Sept. 12.

Zelizer, B. (1993) Journalists as interpretive communities. *Critical Studies in Mass Communication*, 10, 219–237.

5

A Conflict of Media Roles: Advertising, Public Relations, and Journalism

Introduction

In this chapter we examine and evaluate the relationship between different types of media communication, in particular, journalism, advertising, and public relations. Is this a case of an unholy alliance? How can these different modes of transmitting information with different and potentially conflicting objectives and roles be so closely aligned? Where the alignment is purposeful and planned, does it constitute a collusion of unethical complicity? Advertorials (advertisements masquerading as editorial comment) may be viewed as an example of such unethical complicity. The use of advertising or of public relations media releases as a form of propaganda by governments to manipulate or influence public opinion seems equally ethically problematic.

For if the communication of accurate, true, and fair information can potentially come into conflict with the demands of successful

Media, Markets, and Morals, First Edition. Edward H. Spence, Andrew Alexandra, Aaron Quinn, and Anne Dunn.
© 2011 Edward H. Spence, Andrew Alexandra, Aaron Quinn, and Anne Dunn. Published 2011 by Blackwell Publishing Ltd.

persuasion, then the two principles operating within both advertising and public relations, those of information and persuasion, are locked in an *inherent conflict of interests*, or at least a potential conflict. Finally, we raise the issue that we discuss in greater detail in Chapter 6: is the conflict of media roles between journalism on the one hand, and advertising and public relations on the other, conducive to corruption, specifically the corruption of the dissemination of information to the public?

The chapter concludes by showing that journalists cannot allow themselves to treat the public as simply advertising or public relations consumers since the roles of journalism on the one hand, and the roles of advertising and public relations on the other, are inherently incompatible both epistemologically and ethically. Thus journalists cannot compromise their professional role by being in any way involved in the production or dissemination of misleading or deceptive advertorials or infomercials.

Journalism, Advertising, and Public Relations: An Unholy Alliance?

Does the close relationship and association between journalism, advertising, and public relations in the process of media communication constitute an "unholy alliance" that raises ethical concerns? To answer this question we must first determine what the generic professional or institutional role of each of the three communication mediums is. This will assist us in ascertaining the role morality of each medium in order to determine if those roles are professionally and ethically compatible. For any ethical concerns that may arise from the association of these different communication media may be the result of the association of professionally and ethically incompatible roles. More specifically, ethical concerns may arise as a result of the ambiguity or the blurring of these roles with the result that consumers and citizens are either unaware or uncertain whether the source of the information communicated to them is independent editorial fact, comment or opinion, or a paid-for advertisement or public relations media release.[1]

What are the primary generic roles of journalism, advertising, and public relations?

The primary generic role of *journalism* is to convey information, ideas, and opinions to the public that are either of interest to the public or of public interest.[2] Journalism should inform citizens and animate democracy. It should do so with honesty, fairness, independence, and respect for the rights of others. Its agents should strive for objectivity, without allowing personal or commercial interests to undermine accuracy, justice, or impartiality. Two of the primary fundamental principles of journalism are truth and the right of the public to be informed on matters of public interest.[3]

The primary generic role of *advertising* is to present products or services in ways that enhance their marketability and makes consumers more favorably disposed towards those products or services with the ultimate objective of promoting their sale.

The primary generic role of *public relations* is to mediate or facilitate information between PR clients and the clients' targeted audiences and/or the general public through various media outlets. The ultimate objective of this role is to present the PR clients in a favorable light, or at least in a less unfavorable light, to their targeted audiences and/or the general public.

What are the minimal primary professional and instrumental requirements for achieving those roles?

In the case of *journalism*, the information conveyed to the public must be independent, balanced, fair, unbiased, accurate, true, and as far as possible objective. Opinions must be clearly and unambiguously demarcated from facts and other advertising and public relations material.

In *advertising*, the advertisements promoting the products or services to the consumers must be effectively persuasive.

As for *public relations*, the PR campaigns and strategies addressed to the public on behalf of clients must be persuasive and influential in creating a positive impression of the clients, or at least in minimizing any negative impressions about the clients, in the minds of the targeted audiences and/or the public.

Are those roles and their realization compatible with each other?

Journalism and advertising By the avowed principles of journalism, *journalistic information* must meet the standards of balance, fairness, honesty, independence, truth, accuracy, objectivity, disclosure of all essential facts, avoidance of distorting emphasis, and avoidance of unnecessary emphasis on personal characteristics (race, gender, ethnicity, etc.). Personal interest or advertising and commercial considerations must not undermine accuracy, fairness, or independence. Pictures and sounds presented in publications must be true and accurate.

To the extent that most, if not all, of the above journalistic standards and principles are *not* applicable because they are not relevant to advertising, then the roles of journalism and advertising are significantly different and potentially incompatible. As argued by Edward Spence and Brett van Heekeren (2005, chs 6 and 8) truth, independence, objectivity, and the absence of distorting emphasis are usually not relevant to advertising, which often relies on metaphor, fiction, and fantasy rather than facts in its communication strategies. If the primary objective of advertising is effective *persuasion* and that of journalism *information* (which, as we saw in Chapter 2, must be true or at least truthful), we can see how those two primary objectives can potentially come into opposition and result in a conflict of interests or conflict of roles.[4] For insofar as the primary ultimate objective of advertising is the successful promotion or placement of consumer products or services in order to persuade consumers to purchase them, effective persuasion need not have any of the traditional epistemological characteristics of journalistic information.

Persuasion strategies, as the dominant communication strategies used in advertising, can succeed just as effectively and sometimes even more so in persuading consumers to feel predisposed towards the products or services advertised. An appeal to consumers' desires, fears, aspirations, fantasies, and other emotions makes an appeal to factual, truthful, unbiased, and objective information appear, by comparison, irrelevant or redundant.

Journalism, public relations, and advertising The primary role of public relations is to manage the communication of information on behalf of its clients with the ultimate objective of influencing public opinion in favor of its clients. Like advertising, its primary operative principle is persuasion. Public relations information is used mainly as a tool or strategy of persuasion. Like advertising, public relations seeks primarily to make its targeted audiences favorably predisposed, or at least less unfavorably disposed, towards its clients' products or services. And similarly as with advertising, public relations operates with two potentially incompatible and conflicting principles, the principle of information and the principle of persuasion. Unlike journalism, which, in principle, is committed to informing the public truthfully and objectively on matters of public interest, independent of any other commercial interests, public relations, as an advocate for its clients, is primarily committed to informing the public only on matters pertinent to its clients' interests. Moreover it does so in a manner that is partial and favorable to its clients, even if it means "spinning" the truth a little to adjust reality to fit the favorable image they are required to convey to the public on their clients' behalf.

Journalism is committed by its professional role to disseminate information to members of the public, qua citizens, that is concomitant of the *public's interest*. Advertising and public relations, by contrast, are committed by their role as commercial advocates of their clients only to convey information to members of the public, qua consumers, that is concomitant of their *clients' interest*. Such information is at best of interest to the public only derivatively. For the primary interest that advertising and public relations clients have is to create a good impression of themselves and of their products and services in the minds of consumers. This is so whether the consumption relates to products or to information.

The following analysis of advertorials is a key example of how the two principles of persuasion and information, which are present in both advertising and public relations, can lead to a potential conflict of interests or roles. This may be detrimental to the public in their dual roles as both consumers and citizens. Advertorials are an illustration of an inherent epistemological and ethical incompatibility between journalism on the one hand, and advertising or public relations on the other. They constitute, in effect, a complicity of deception generated by the covert and unheralded mixing of journalistic informational practices with those of advertising or public relations persuasion practices. The following discussion will focus primarily on how advertorials raise potential and actual ethical problems for both journalism and advertising.

The Problem of Advertorials

The *inherent problem* with advertorials is the combining of two modes of communication that are epistemologically incompatible, journalism and advertising.

The *ethical problem* with advertorials is that they are designed to deceive. They rely on the epistemological credence of journalistic information to make the advertising more credible and reliable in the eyes and ears of the consumers. Part of that deception has to do with the *approach problem*, which involves advertorials seeking to communicate with consumers by stealth: approaching them not as consumers but as citizens who are purportedly being informed on some matter of public interest. This problem also highlights the inherent epistemological and ethical incompatibility of journalism and advertising as media of communication, for journalism approaches its audience as *citizens* whereas advertising approaches its audience as *consumers.*

Advertising Laws: Cash for Comment

In what has come to be known in Australia as the the "cash for comment" case, John Laws, a well-known commercial radio celebrity, abused his editorial power for the purpose of influencing the opinion of his two-million strong audience favorably towards a group of banks for a sum of A$1.2 million. The financial transaction between Laws and the banks was carried out in secret and concealed from the public, including his audience. Just a few weeks prior to his deal with the banks, Laws had repeatedly criticized them on his 2UE radio program, a commercial station in Sydney, for acting unethically in imposing unjustified bank fees on customers while simultaneously cutting back on vital services, especially in rural areas. However, a few days later and following his secret deal with the banks, Laws suddenly changed his tune from combative and cutting criticism to mellifluous conciliatory comments about the banks which, he said, "are not that bad after all."

John Laws' favorable comments on the banks following his deal with them can be seen as a typical instance of an advertorial. Advertorials are advertisements masquerading as editorials (editorial comment or opinion). In the case of advertorials, the difference between advertising and editorial comment is often blurred to the advantage of the advertisers and their clients. The public would have been led to think Laws was expressing a genuinely unbiased and informed honest view about the banks when in fact and unbeknown to his listeners he was advertising the banks' "merits" for a price, offering editorial comment for cash. In the United States the "cash for editorial comment" phenomenon is known as "payola."

In the above case, we are able to observe an important distinction between the dictates of advertising versus those of journalism: *external* versus *internal instrumentalism.* In *external instrumentalism,* "the means or instrument is external to the end, in that it need not have any of the distinctive characteristics of the end. In *internal instrumentalism,*" by contrast, the means or instrument is internal to the end: it is instrumental to the end not merely as causal means but also intrinsically in that its features are also constitutive of the end. It serves as an instrument to the end by bringing about a certain result, while at the same time it has the distinctive characteristics of the result (Gewirth 1986, 295). To illustrate the difference between internal and external instrumentalism, Gewirth gives the example of a "lecture on some scientific or philosophical topic":

> If the lecture is delivered simply or mainly in order to earn money, then the lecture, as means or instrument, is external to the end: spreading enlightenment or understanding on scientific or philo-sophical topics is conceptually distinct from earning money, since each can be done without the other. If, on the other hand, the lecture is delivered for the purpose of improving its hearers' understanding of the topics with which it deals, then the lecture, as means or instrument, is internal to the end: the very process of presenting the relevant intellectual considerations exhibits and conforms to the same intellectual criteria as constitute the end of improving the understanding of the subject matter. (Gewirth 1986, 295–296)

In the case of advertorials what we have is a conflict between internal instrumentalism and external instrumentalism. In journal-ism, its means or instrument of communicating information to the public truthfully and fairly is *internal* to its end of informing the public on matters of public interest. By contrast, in advertising, whose main purpose is the successful persuasion of consumers to purchase a range of products or services, the means or instrument of communicating information to the public on those products and services is *external* to its end of providing information to the public.

In the case of journalism, both the means and the end of com-municating information conform to the same conceptual and pro-fessional criteria of providing true and fair information to the public. By contrast, in the case of advertising the strategy of informing the public about consumer products or services as a means of persuading them to buy them is external to the provision of information, and sometimes even irrelevant. For the end of communicating information so as to provide knowledge to consumers about products or services is conceptually distinct from the means of informing them for the mere purpose of persuading them to buy products or services. Moreover, unlike information that of necessity must be true or truthful (see Chapter 2), persuasion need not be true or truthful.[5] For misinformation through half-truths, lies, and deception can be just as effectively persuasive as the truth, and sometimes even more so, in advertising.

The above discussion of advertorials should alert us to how conflicts of roles and principles across different professions or institutions, whose professional and institutional instrumentalism can be at odds with each other, can result in unethical practices, as in the John Laws "cash for comment" case study. Such practices can prove detrimental to the public through their being misinformed on matters of public interest. It is because of the importance that professional and institutional roles have in the determination of role morality (see Chapter 2), that those roles should be clearly defined, demarcated, and understood by all stakeholders. For quite often unethical practices are the result of an ambiguity, or in the most extreme cases ignorance, of what one's professional, institutional, or other socially determined role is. Moreover, unethical practices can and do arise because of uncertainty or ignorance as to how one's intra-professional role interrelates with and sometimes comes into conflict with other professional roles in the media, which typically operates across increasingly convergent roles in the marketplace of information. When confronted with the "cash for comment" charge, John Laws' defensive response was to claim something along the lines that he was "an entertainer not a journalist and so journalistic standards didn't have an ethical hook on him" (ABC, *Media Watch*, 1999).

It was correctly pointed out to Laws, however, that the crucial factor was not what *he* thought his role was when offering favorable comments about the banks but what his *audience* thought his role was. Most if not all the members of his 2UE radio audience would have been led to believe that Laws was expressing his own informed and honest opinion about the banks and not running a paid advertisement for them. So, naturally, they would have thought Laws' role to be that of someone who, like a journalist, offers objective comment or opinion on some important issue. He was therefore ethically committed to that perceived role. This was a perception he encouraged by concealing the payment of $1.2 million he had received from the banks for advocating their cause.

Another example of role ambiguity is the ambiguity relating to the role of public relations practitioners as mediators or facilitators of paid-for communication that can potentially result in unethical practices. Functioning as advertorials or infomercials, public relations *media releases*,[6] which are produced and disseminated on behalf of paying clients, appear as editorial pieces in newspapers or other media publications, sometimes with a journalist's byline at the end of entirely unaltered press releases. Like advertorials, these media releases amount to deception. And as in advertising, so too in public relations, the purpose of communicating information through persuasion strategies on behalf of paying clients is incompatible with the true role of communicating information. For that role must be truthful, since information of necessity must be true and accurate, whether or not it seeks to be persuasive.

To see more clearly how the *role moralities* of the different media fit in with the *internal and external instrumentalism* that applies to them, consider the following argument. We have seen that the primary role of information is to provide the public, either as citizens or as consumers, with knowledge about something, for example, news, products, and services. In the case of journalism, whose primary role is to inform the public on matters of public interest, the *instrumental role* of information (of providing knowledge) and the role morality of journalism (of providing information to the public) are on the same page. Both roles are instrumentally internal since they are means to the same end – the end of providing knowledge. Moreover, those instrumental means are internal to that end and have the same characteristics as that end since the means (information) and the end (knowledge) are of the same kind. Both must be true or truthful. By contrast, in the case of advertising and public relations, the instrumental role of information (of providing knowledge) and the role moralities of advertising and public relations are not on the same page, or at least need not be on the same page, as they are for journalism. This is because the primary but not exclusive role of advertising and public relations is to persuade rather than to inform. Information is merely an instrumentally external means to their ultimate end of persuasion. Moreover, the *means* of informing does not have the same characteristics as the *end* of persuasion. Information must of necessity be true whereas persuasion need not be so. Propaganda can be persuasive without being true.

In sum, as a means of informing, editorial comment is congruent with its end of providing information to the public. By contrast, public relations media releases that seek to emulate editorial comment through the guise of infomercials are merely externally instrumental to the end of providing information and often antithetical to the essence of information understood as a type of knowledge, which of necessity has to be true or truthful. Notice that if the role of information in the process of communication is to impart knowledge both the means and the end of that role must be the same. The means must track the end and the end must be responsive to the means. This at least is what is meant to happen when journalism operates as it ought to: conveying information to the public on matters of public interest and matters that are of interest to the public. That is its role morality (Chapter 2). By contrast the role of advertising and public relations as a form of advocacy on behalf of paying clients is to convey information with the aim of persuasion. Those are the respective role moralities of advertising and of public relations as industries of persuasion. The information conveyed by them can of course be true but need not be so, and as in the John Laws case study and the case study that follows, messages of persuasion masquerading as information are often conveyed to consumers in misleading and deceptive ways, by commission as well as by omission. For if the primary role of those industries is to persuade rather than to inform, then the means of persuading need not be congruent with the misleadingly presumed and avowed end of providing "information" on products, services, or clients for the benefit of the public.

A Collusion of Deception

In April 2005 the Australian Broadcasting Corporation's *Media Watch* television program presented "Media Drug Dupes" a story involving a campaign to deceive the Australian public. The campaign was orchestrated by an Australian public relations consultancy firm on behalf of its client, Abbott Australasia, a pharmaceutical company. This PR firm, let's refer to it as XYZ, targeted several regional newspapers around Australia. Its strategic intention was that these newspapers, given their known limited staff resources, would publish its press releases concerning a new drug to treat obesity as journalistic opinion pieces. They did. This is a well-known and pervasive PR strategy that targets and uses journalists as "credible third-party endorsers" of their clients' paid-for information. Of course the public on the receiving end of such information remains, in the absence of a qualifying statement that these are press releases, unaware that the information presented to them as journalistic comment or opinion is, quite often, a word-for-word press release. And in some cases, it is accompanied by a journalist's byline for extra credibility.

According to the *Media Watch* program the Abbott press release appeared verbatim as news in the *Perth Sunday Times* (November 21, 2004), the *Manning River Times* (February 4–5, 2005), and the *Central Coast Sun Weekly* in New South Wales (December 16, 2004), without an acknowledgment in any of these publications that this was, in fact, a press release.

Given the above information on the Abbott case, and on the basis that deception and manipulation are prima facie ethically objectionable, we can now determine if the practice of passing off press releases as news or journalistic comment or opinion is unethical.

In the case of the journalists and their newspapers who knowingly or negligently presented Abbott's press releases as independent comment in journalistic columns designed to look like news, our answer is affirmative. For journalists are ethically and professionally committed by their own avowed code of ethics (in Australia, the Media and Entertainment Arts Alliance Code of Ethics) to provide information to the public on matters of public interest in an honest, objective, fair, and as far as possible accurate manner, without allowing commercial or other biased interests to interfere with those principles; specifically, the two fundamental principles of journalism, *truth* and *the public's right to know* (MEAA Code of Ethics). The journalists and their organizations that misrepresented Abbott's press releases as news acted unethically because they misinformed the public about a matter of public interest. Clearly, obesity, as an important issue of public health, is a matter of public interest.

But what if the information contained in Abbott's press release was by and large accurate? Let us assume for the sake of argument that it was. By disseminating that information to the public, weren't the journalists and their organizations fulfilling their ethical obligation under the MEAA code of ethics of informing the public accurately on a matter of public interest? The answer is no. The simple reason is that "information" as a type of knowledge must not only be true or at least truthful but it must also meet the general epistemic criteria of objectivity including those of independence, reliability, and hence credibility of the source of that information. Even if it were true, the information in Abbott's press release lacked objective justification. For there was no independent, reliable, and hence credible corroborating evidence that the information provided by Abbott through its press release was accurate. Therefore, in the absence of any other independent information from a credible source corroborating Abbott's information, the information it provided in its press release, which was reproduced verbatim by journalists and their organizations, lacked objectivity and therefore epistemic credence. Thus the journalists and their organizations failed in their ethical duty of exercising due epistemic diligence in presenting information to the public, which to the best of their knowledge was objective and credible.

The opposite was in fact true. They must have known, or ought to have known, that the information reproduced from Abbott's press release and published as news lacked credibility, for it lacked corroborating evidence from a credible independent source. Moreover, the journalists and their organizations knew or ought to have known that readers of their papers would have accepted the Abbott press releases, which had been presented as "news," at face value and in good faith and so would have been misled and deceived. Even on the assumption that the information contained in Abbott's press release was accurate, its presentation as news was a deception and thus ethically objectionable. Moreover, as argued above, even if it were accurate it wouldn't count as reliable and credible information as it lacked objectivity and independence.

Additionally, the deception of presenting a press release as news to their readers makes the deception by the journalists and their organizations a serious breach of a duty of trust. This undermines the communication of information process by which the public as citizens are informed by journalists about matters of public interest. A professional duty of trust owed by journalists to the public to inform, and not misinform, them is enshrined in almost all journalistic codes of ethics around the world including that of Australia. For example, the Australian MEAA code of ethics states clearly and unequivocally that:

> Respect for truth and the public's right to information are fundamental principles of journalism ... They scrutinise power, but also exercise it, and should be accountable. Accountability engenders trust. Without trust, journalists do not fulfil their public responsibilities. Alliance members engaged in journalism commit themselves to
> > Honesty
> > Fairness
> > Independence
> > Respect for the rights of others.

Journalists are thus morally obliged not to deceive the public by disseminating press releases designed to look like editorial comment or news, as in the Abbott case. To the extent that they do, they act unethically and abuse their duty of trust to inform the public truthfully and objectively in a fair and balanced manner.

What about the PR consultants who produced the press releases? Did they also act unethically? Insofar as the PR firm XYZ knowingly designed and placed the press releases on Abbott's behalf with the strategic intention that they be used as journalistic comment in the targeted regional newspapers, the answer is yes. The design of press releases to be read as journalistic columns targeted at newspapers that do not possess the resources for rewriting them after proper, independent corroboration and disclosure of their source is, as mentioned earlier, a well-known and widespread practice for at least some, if not most, PR practitioners. However, even if the journalistic resources for rewriting press releases after independent verification of their content are not available, doesn't the ultimate ethical responsibility of not presenting PR press releases as news lie with the journalists and not with the PR practitioners who provide the press releases?

Granted that journalists do have the ultimate responsibility, as indeed they do, PR practitioners themselves are not free from all moral responsibility. For to the extent that the public is subjected to deception as a result of the PR strategy of presenting, through the collaboration of lazy or unscrupulous journalists, press releases as journalistic comment, the PR practitioners responsible for producing and disseminating those press releases are party to the deception. Hence, they are culpable of unethical professional conduct. For their designed intention and their consequent actions in putting that design into practice is that their press releases are used in that way. A person who makes available a weapon to another person knowing that he or she will use the weapon to violate the rights of another is party to that violation and is thus ethically culpable, even if the greatest moral responsibility falls ultimately on the person who pulls the trigger. We have shown that XYZ, and PR practitioners who engage in similar tactics, are party to the deception, and we have begun with the assumption that deception is fundamentally unethical. But this is far from a case of judging one professional or institutional body inappropriately against the ethical imperatives of another, since XYZ and PR practitioners of their ilk contravene their own code of ethics. For the code of ethics of the Public Relations

Institute of Australia (PRIA) clearly states that "members shall not knowingly disseminate false or misleading information and shall take care to avoid doing so inadvertently."[7] XYZ broke this rule by knowingly, or at least negligently, allowing their media releases to be used by journalists in a misleading manner. Even if the content were true, its presentation as objective findings produced by disinterested and independent journalists was not. It was, in other words, not truthful.

However, even if the practice of producing press releases designed to be used as journalistic comment is unethical, does it, as in the case of journalists, constitute a breach of trust? The answer to this question is based squarely on whether that practice involves the abuse of a duty of trust, a key duty owed by professional communicators to those with whom they seek to communicate. In the present case, the relevant duty of trust owed by PR practitioners to the public is not to deceive them, especially on matters of public interest.

The problem for establishing whether such a duty of trust is professionally owed by PR practitioners to the general public is exacerbated by the ill-defined and not well-understood professional role (assuming it is a professional role) of public relations. This is a complex issue, well beyond the scope of the present chapter. Suffice it to say, that PR practitioners themselves see one of their roles as "building, nurturing, and maintaining organization–public relationships ..." (Bruning and Ledingham 1999, 158). All professional relationships must be based on trust, for a necessary condition for all morally sound communicative relationships is respect for the rights of the relevant parties within such relationships. Those rights require that the participating parties in those relationships not deceive each other. It is therefore reasonable to argue that deceptive practices such as the production of press releases by PR practitioners for the strategic intention of disseminating them to media organizations to be used as journalistic comment constitute a breach and abuse of trust. This, together with the quasi-avowed ethical responsibility stated in the PRIA code of ethics that "members shall not knowingly disseminate false or misleading information and shall take care to avoid doing so inadvertently," may suffice to establish a quasi-duty of trust: a duty of trust owed by PR practitioners to the public not to deceive them. Thus, press releases designed and produced by PR practitioners to be disseminated as news or journalistic comment or opinion constitute a breach of trust, specifically, a breach of trust that undermines the information and communication process.

In sum, both advertorials and infomercials, in the form of media releases presented by journalists as "news" without any acknowledgment that these are media releases, involve two opposing principles. In their intent to appear as editorial comment, they embody the *principle of information*, which requires information to be true, truthful, and justified through independent corroboration and verification. On the other hand, as a form of paid-for advertisements or public relations media releases, they embody the *principle of persuasion*. This principle does not necessarily require the information communicated to be true, truthful, or even justified. Of course information that is true and justified can and often is persuasive. However, persuasion need not necessarily be achieved through information that meets the condition of truth since misinformation, half-truths, and lies can just as easily be persuasive if presented in the right format. Successful propaganda is a case in point. Another way of making the same point is as follows: if the primary purpose of communication is to persuade, then the "information" communicated need not be true. It can, of course, be true but it need not. By contrast, if the primary purpose of communication is to inform by imparting knowledge, then the information communicated must of necessity be true or at least intended to be true. So whereas truth and truthfulness are *intrinsic and necessary* to the communication of information, they are only *extrinsic and contingent* to communication by way of persuasion. In the case of communicating information for imparting knowledge, truth is *internal* to the process of communication whereas truth is at best *external* in the case of communicating information for the purpose of persuasion. Clearly, then, the notion of *internal instrumentalism* applies to and fits in with communication by way of information whereas, by contrast, external instrumentalism applies to and fits in with communication by way of persuasion.

Interestingly, the ambiguity of the role of public relations, and the question of whether or not it is a profession, make it difficult to determine what the public relations industry's fiduciary duties of trust are and to whom they are owed. For example, does the public relations industry as communicator of information have a fiduciary duty to the public for ensuring that the information mediated by them to the public through the media is accurate, true, and fair? If the answer to the question is yes, then the public relations industry faces a conflict of interests or roles that is inherent to its own practice. For if the communication of accurate, true, and fair information can potentially come into conflict with the demands of successful persuasion, then the two principles operating within public relations, those of information and persuasion, are locked in an *inherent conflict of interests*, or at least a potential conflict. To the extent that this is the case, then, the practice of public relations is by virtue of the nature of this inherent conflict prone to unethical conduct, that is, the practice of mediating or facilitating information that relates to matters of public interest for the self-regarding gain of the public relations practitioners and their clients but to the detriment of the public.

Citizens and Consumers

Citizens require information to enable them to make informed decisions about important issues of public interest, which affect or could potentially affect their rights to freedom and well-being. To that end, citizens, collectively the public, have a right to such information and that right is rationally supported and justified, as we saw in Chapters 2 and 3, by the principle of generic consistency (PGC). That information must be true, balanced, fair, accurate, and objective. To that end, the source of that information must be independent, credible, and reliable. In their role as providers of information to the public on matters of public interest, journalists are thus committed to those epistemological values. Their journalistic or press freedom to inform the public on matters of public interest, and also less significantly on matters that are of interest to the public, is conditional on the journalists' professional and ethical obligation to inform the public according to those epistemological and ethical values and standards.

By contrast, as consumers, people are provided with information that is primarily designed to persuade them to consume products (advertising), services, comments, or other packaged information in favor of particular individuals, corporations, or institutions (public relations).

In their avowed role as providers of information to the public on matters of public interest, journalists cannot allow themselves to treat the public as advertising or public relations consumers since the roles of journalism and the roles of advertising and public relations are inherently epistemologically and ethically incompatible. Thus journalists cannot compromise their professional role by being in any way involved in the production or dissemination of advertorials or infomercials.

Advertorials that seek to influence public policy or to exert influence on matters of public interest undermine the independent and fair flow of information, which in turn undermines the democratic process which relies for its effectiveness on an informed citizenry. To the extent that they interfere with the free and independent flow of information on matters of public interest, they are a form of subversive and unethical censorship.

The fundamental difference between journalism on the one hand, and advertising and public relations on the other, is that the former, according to its own avowed role, seeks to approach the public primarily as citizens whereas the latter seek to approach the public primarily as consumers of products, services, and even information. Advertising and public relations' respective presentations of "information" often fail the conditions of knowledge that characterize or should characterize information owing to the absence of truth and epistemological independence and objectivity. By contrast, to the extent that journalistic information meets the requirements of truth

113

and epistemological independence and objectivity, it can qualify as a type of knowledge.

Advertorials and Conflict of Interest

Pay for Play

Why does radio suck? Because most stations play only the songs the record companies pay them to. And things are going to get worse. (Boehlert 2001)

"Payola" is a combination of two words: "pay" and "Victrola" (LP record player) and has its official origins in the 1960s when on May 9, 1960 rock radio pioneer Alan Freed was convicted of accepting bribes to play particular records and fined. Before Freed's conviction, payola was not illegal but after Freed's trial anti-payola laws were passed that made payola illegal. More recently Joe Isgro, a well-known independent record promoter known as an "indie," fought payola-related charges for almost a decade before the charges were dismissed in 1996. Isgro's story about the shady world of independent record promoters or indies who act as middlemen between record companies and radio stations to promote the playing of songs on radio stations is told in Dannen (1991).

Indies align themselves with particular radio stations and undertake to pay the stations "promotional payments" that can amount to hundreds of thousands of dollars a year. The indies get paid anything from US$1,000 to $2,000 by the record company that owns the label every time a radio station plays a song on the indies' pay-list. In a $12 billion-a-year music industry, almost every commercial radio station has an indie. With 10,000 commercial radio stations in the United States it is clear that the money exchanged between record companies and radio stations through indies runs into many millions of dollars a year. Some indies make about $1 million a year (nice work if you can get it!). And it's all legal as long as the radio stations disclose to their listeners the sponsorship money from promotional payments that stations receive from record companies through their indies. Whether the required disclosure is made, however, and to what degree and how effectively it is policed by the Federal Communications Commission (FCC) is a different matter. With so many songs on air at any one time, the task of disclosure and monitoring of disclosure becomes practically impossible. The crucial question is: how many of the millions of people who listen to the radio each day know of this cozy financial relationship between the record producers, the indies, and the radio stations? If they are not told, and the chances are that in most cases they are not, they are none the wiser about the largely hidden financial deals behind the air waves.

Record stations claim that indies don't call the tunes that get played but simply allow the indies to furnish them with promotional lists of songs for consideration and that the radio station has the final say in what gets played. However, when stations can have $100,000 or more revenue coming in from a record company through its indie middleman, it is difficult to believe that indies are given access to the stations but exercise no influence as to what songs go on air. Depending on the size of the radio station, $100,000-plus a year can buy a lot of influence, let alone access. At least that would be a reasonable impression for an independent observer to form. At the very least, a radio station that accepts money for playing records is involved in a conflict of interest since its judgment on what songs it plays will be seen to be biased towards the songs it gets paid to play rather than those that may merit play but can't afford to pay.[8]

The above case study and the "cash for comment" case involving the radio personality John Laws illustrate both the inherent conflicting nature of advertorials and how they can potentially result in unethical conduct, which misleads and deceives the public. In Laws' case his commenting favorably on the banks, qua independent and objective journalistic commentator, without informing his audience that he was being paid handsomely to do so, qua advertiser, constituted deception and hence was ethically reprehensible. Similarly, the case of payola-like play-for-pay practices by commercial radio stations in the United States constitutes deception and thus unethical conduct even if the transactions are otherwise legal. For the radio listeners are not adequately informed through transparent, full disclosure that the play of songs on their air waves is being paid for by the record companies that own the labels.

Notice, however, that the mere disclosure of advertorials and payola-like arrangements between record companies and radio stations does not remove the conflict of interest that these commercial arrangements involve, though, if disclosed, it does make them ethically unobjectionable by removing the factor that makes advertorials ethically objectionable in the first place, namely, their potential for deception. For if cash-for-comment and pay-for-play arrangements have a tendency to impact on and to influence the proper exercise of judgment of radio commentators offering opinions or comments on matters of public interest – such as matters involving banks, or of radio disc-jockeys selecting songs to be played on the air waves – then the conflict of interest remains, even after it has been disclosed.

However, notwithstanding its disclosure, conflicts of interest involved in advertorials remain ethically problematic. That is because the air waves are a public space which commercial radios use to inform the public on matters that are both of interest to the public, such as music for example, and of public interest, such as banks. If the public cannot rely on the epistemological credibility of the sources of that information because the sources are biased towards commercial sponsors who have paid the radio stations for their comments and the play of their songs, then the information that is communicated to the public is censored, censored by the agendas and interests of the commercial sponsors that may not coincide with what is of interest to the public or what is of public interest.

Commercial radio stations use the ambiguity of their role as providers of information and entertainment to communicate with the public qua citizens for the primary objective of selling products to the public qua consumers, in the form of news, commentary, or songs which have been paid for by commercial sponsors that effectively censor what the public should hear and know. And the information the public receives by commercial radio, in the main, is not the unencumbered honest, objective, and epistemologically independent opinions of the commentators and disc jockeys but those of their paymasters, the commercial sponsors that pull the strings of the puppet-show known as commercial radio.

Advertising as Propaganda

Liberal Ads to Influence Voting

The Liberals, one of the two major and dominant political parties in Australia, the other being the Labor party, ran advertisements claiming that big business was leaving the state of Victoria because of union militancy (Australian 2002). They did so in the hope of influencing the Victorian electorate to vote for the Liberal party in the 2002 state elections. However, to the embarrassment of the party, a number of businesses that featured in the advertisements came forward to deny the allegations. They claimed that they were not consulted about the allegations and that they had not given their consent to be featured in the controversial advertisements. At least six companies demanded that their names be removed from the Liberal advertising that linked job losses to union militancy while another three refuted claims that factory closures were related to union unrest. Nokia, one of the companies featured in the advertisements denied claims that it had laid off staff because of union trouble. While admitting that it had laid off staff in Victoria, Nokia insisted this was owing to a global downturn in business rather than as a result of union trouble. However, despite these denials and after dropping the offending ads that had featured the complainants who claimed the allegations were not true, the Liberals stuck to their tune. They continued to run advertisements claiming that business was being driven out of Victoria because of union unrest. In politics as in advertising, it seems truth is not allowed to spoil a good story.

The above case study illustrates the dangers to the democratic process of governments or political parties using advertising as

117

a form of propaganda to "inform" the public on matters of public interest. In the attempt to persuade the electorate in Victoria not to vote for the incumbent Labor party, the Liberals resorted to propaganda by means of misinformation propagated though false, or at least inaccurate, advertising against the trade unions (which, in Australia, are traditionally aligned with the Labor party). They did so for the sole purpose of discrediting the Labor party in Victoria and influencing the election result in favor of their own party. Fortunately for the Victorian electorate, the media, fulfilling its avowed journalistic role of watchdog, exposed the falsehood or at least inaccuracy of the Liberal advertisements, emphasizing once more the all-important role that a free and independent press plays in a democratic system.

It is precisely because of the important and crucial journalistic role that the media play in a democracy, as providers of independent and objective information to the public on matters of public interest, that the role of journalism should be protected – protected, that is, from potentially conflicting commercial and political interests. For such interests may bias that role in favor of behind-the-scenes powerful commercial sponsors. This has the effect of manipulating the media as an instrument of misinformation and propaganda, so as to further the interests of the commercial sponsors rather than the interests of the public or the public interest. Even when those commercial strings are disclosed, their disclosure as we saw does not necessarily remove the conflict of interest, for it still has the tendency to bias media opinion and comment in favor of the commercial sponsors to the detriment of the public. Hence, it is important and crucial that media organizations, which are seen by their audiences as fulfilling the journalistic role, protect that role from any commercially induced bias. They can do so by not mixing together, and in one breath, cash and comment or play for pay. Editorial comment and opinion should thus be free and independent of any advertising or public relations, whether hidden or declared. Like oil and water they just don't mix.

Conclusion

The use of advertorials can be an effective strategy for advertising a product or a service because of their ability to convey advertising material in the concealed form of an editorial comment or opinion, which carries much greater epistemological weight than a mere advertisement. If the ultimate goal of advertising is to persuade consumers to feel favorably predisposed towards the advertised products or services, or at least not to feel unfavorably predisposed towards them, then the use of advertorials to promote products or services is an effective persuasive strategy. Hence, advertorials are in keeping with the ultimate goal of advertising and are therefore instrumentally desirable in fulfilling that goal.

However, even if advertorials are instrumentally desirable in meeting the ultimate goal of advertising, the instrumental cost from any potential fall-out when this type of deceptive practice is exposed may outweigh any short-term instrumental benefit, one that may accrue as a result of the use of advertorials as an advertising strategy. So the use of advertorials instrumentally as an advertising strategy may not be beneficial and hence not desirable in the long term.

But even if the use of advertorials may prove instrumentally desirable in the short term for a particular advertiser, they may prove instrumentally undesirable for the advertising industry over-all because they bring the industry into disrepute. As a result of the John Laws "cash for comment" scandal, the commercial radio industry in Australia was in the public mind smeared by the same ethically unclean brush. The advertising industry has, therefore, an ethical responsibility to its ethically bound members and to the public at large to ensure that this type of activity is properly regulated, through adequate penalties for ethical infringements by individual members.

As advertorials are a form of deception and deception is unethical (with the exception of some limited cases of justified deception for the greater good of society, such as undercover police and inves-tigative journalistic work), their use in advertising is ethically undesirable. Inaccurate if not false information, in the form of government advertising, can prove detrimental, both for the source of the information as well as for its intended targeted audience as illustrated by the case study "Liberal Ads to Influence Voting" (see above). Therefore advertising in the form of government propaganda that misinforms the public, either intentionally or by negligence, is ethically undesirable, even if this type of advertising is instrumentally desirable for the advertiser and the government, at least in the short term.

However, a merely instrumental benefit is a two-edged sword. It can potentially harm the beneficiary of the instrumental benefit if it backfires. Perhaps as a result of the scandal surrounding the inaccurate information provided to the Victorian electorate by the Liberal party through its pre-election advertising campaign, the Labor party won the elections in Victoria by a landslide. The moral of this story is not to throw mud against the wind just in case it lands on your own face. Overall then, inaccurate information through advertising in the form of government propaganda is both ethically and instrumentally undesirable.

Taking all instrumental and ethical considerations into account, the overall deceptive and misleading advertising practices in the form of advertorials or infomercials – including advertising strategies that disseminate inaccurate information in the form of propaganda or misleading public relations practices in the form of media release journalism – are on balance both instrumentally and ethically undesirable. They should therefore be avoided. Moreover, even on the supposition that they are somehow in keeping with the role morality of the professions that practice them, namely, advertising and public relations, these practices violate the pre-scriptions of universal public morality. They violate the legitimate rights of citizens not to be misinformed, especially on matters of public interest. The practices are therefore unethical. As we saw in Chapter 2, when there is a conflict between them, universal public morality always trumps role morality.

Finally, where the collusion of journalism and advertising or public relations – in the form of advertorials, cash for comment, and public relations media releases – results in misinformation, such collusion can be said to be conducive to *media corruption*. We will examine this topic in more detail in the next chapter. Indeed, some forms of institutional and industrial types of media corruption, as we shall discuss in Chapter 6, are the result of collusion resulting from conflicting media roles.

Chapter study questions

1. The following case study is reproduced from the Center for Media and Democracy website (http://www.prwatch.org/node/3603, accessed Apr. 15, 2010). Using the analysis in the chapter concerning the problematic nature of advertorials, identify and evaluate the ethical issues pertaining to this particular case study? Using the analysis for media corruption in Chapter 6, would you identify and describe this case as an instance of media corruption, and if so, why?

> ### Trust Us, We're Paid TV Experts!
>
> "The use of TV consumer experts is the latest way marketers have tried to disguise their promotions as real news," similar to magazine "'advertorials' designed to look like editorial features" and video news releases aired as TV reports. The stable of paid "experts" includes "Today" show tech-product reviewer Corey Greenberg, "trend and fashion expert" Katlean de Monchy, *Popular Photography & Imaging* magazine editor John Owens, and *Child* magazine tech editor James Oppenheim. The *Wall Street Journal* reports that all four "experts" have neglected to disclose to viewers that they received payments to promote products being discussed. *Journal* reporter James Bandler writes, "TV shows present these gurus' recommendations as unbiased and based solely on their expertise. But that presentation is misleading if the experts have been paid to mention products."

2. What is it about the nature of information that renders the non-disclosure of cash-for-comment cases ethically problematic?
3. Why do advertorials constitute a conflict of interests or a conflict of roles? Even if they do constitute such a conflict, what is ethically wrong with such conflicts?
4. Why is journalism an instance of *internal instrumentalism* whereas advertising and public relations are, by contrast, instances of *external instrumentalism*? How does the distinction between internal and external instrumentalism affect, if at all, the manner in which these different media disseminate information?
5. Is it possible for advertorials and media releases to be ethically unproblematic? How could this be achieved?

Notes

1. The primary generic roles described here are the manifest common roles that emanate from a general social conception and understanding of the respective professional or institutional practices of journalism, advertising, and public relations. Of course it is possible that some of the specific roles and practices of journalism, advertising, and public relations deviate in various ways from the primary generic roles described here. However, insofar as the primary generic roles of these professions or institutions describe in general terms, more or less, what the basic and ultimate roles of these professions or institutions are, then these general descriptions are adequate to our purpose of ascertaining the degree of compatibility between these roles.
2. "Public interest" is any interest which impacts directly or indirectly on the collective rights of freedom and well-being of the public, which comprises all the citizens of a state or a nation locally, and all the citizens of the world (cosmopolitans) globally.
3. The journalistic principles referred to here are those described in the current Australian journalistic code of ethics, the Media and Entertainment Arts Alliance (MEAA) Code of Ethics, but those principles are common to most journalistic codes of ethics, especially those of Western democracies, including the USA.

4. For conflict of interest and conflict of roles conducive to media corruption see Spence (2003).
5. For the relevance of truth and knowledge to advertising, see Spence and Van Heekeren (2005, ch. 6).
6. For a detailed analysis and evaluation of the ethics of media releases see Simmons and Spence (2006).
7. Public Relations Institute of Australia, "Individual code of Ethics." http://www.pria.com.au/membercentre/members&code&of&ethics, accessed Nov. 8, 2010.
8. Most of the information for this case study was sourced from Boehlert (2001).

References

Australian (2002) Firms deny claims in liberal ads. *Australian*, Nov. 27, 4.

Boehlert Eric (2001) Pay for Play. *Salon*, Mar. 14. http://www.salon.com/entertainment/feature/2001/03/14/payola/index.html, accessed Nov. 8, 2010

Bruning, S. D., and Ledingham, J. A. (1999) Relationships between organizations and publics: development of a multi-dimensional organization–public scale. *Public Relations Review*, 25, 157–170.

Dannen, Fredric (1991) *Hit Men: Power Brokers and Fast Money Inside the Music Business*. London: Vintage.

Gewirth, Alan (1986) Professional ethics: the separatist thesis. *Ethics*, 96, 282–300.

Simmons, P., and Spence, E. (2006) The practice and ethics of media release journalism. *Australian Journalism Review*, 28(1), 167–181.

Spence, E. (2003) Conflict of interest and corruption. *Australian Journal of Professional and Applied Ethics*, 5(2), 25–36.

Spence, E., and Van Heekeren, B. (2005) *Advertising Ethics*. Upper Saddle River, NJ: Pearson/Prentice Hall.

6

Corruption in the Media

Introduction

Corruption is one of the most severe and damaging forms of immoral behavior in public and private life, particularly when it involves persons, organizations, and institutions of great social import. The institutions upon which this chapter will focus are mass media, and, in particular, the institution of journalism, which is arguably the media institution of greatest social importance. By no means is this to imply that mass media generally, or journalism more specifically, are comprehensively corrupt institutions; they happen to be one set of many public institutions that suffer from problematic acts of corruption. As we will explain, it appears possible, if not likely, that journalism is at risk of becoming increasingly corrupt because of its economic, social, and – as much as ever – political power. In this chapter, we will analyze instances of wrongdoing, many of which constitute corruption, ranging from

Media, Markets, and Morals, First Edition. Edward H. Spence, Andrew Alexandra, Aaron Quinn, and Anne Dunn.
© 2011 Edward H. Spence, Andrew Alexandra, Aaron Quinn, and Anne Dunn. Published 2011 by Blackwell Publishing Ltd.

the individual behavior of journalists such as Jayson Blair and Jack Kelley; the organizational behavior of media organizations such as the New York Times and Fox News; and industry-wide trends such as editorial interference by non-journalist organizational managers, and the governance of ownership laws that have led to severe ownership concentration.

Though instances and types of corruption are varied and wide-reaching in journalism, one of the most damaging modern forms of journalism corruption comes in the form of news that is embedded in substantial and deliberate political partisanship, one it attempts to conceal. Because most Western news institutions have an important tradition of reporting fairly and impartially – or at least making a good attempt to do so – partisan reporting is especially damaging: audiences expect balanced news but instead they receive partisan news that is deceptively injected into news reports that claim to be, to use Fox News as an example, "fair and balanced."

A contentious and heavily reported instance of what appears to be political partisanship in the news has been Fox News' coverage of 2008 US presidential candidate Rudolph Giuliani's campaign. Though Fox News has long been accused of favoring Republicans in American politics because of its generally right-winged ideology, coverage of Giuliani has been frequently criticized as bald-facedly promotional: highly imbalanced in terms of both the proportion of airtime given to Giuliani compared to other candidates – even other Republicans – and in not mentioning the deep and friendly connections Giuliani has had with News Corp. over the past 20 years (Buettner 2007; Koppelman and Renzas 2007). For example, Giuliani's law partnership represented News Corp. entities in congressional lobbying efforts in 2004–5. Moreover, the head of Fox News, Roger Ailes, worked as Giuliani's media consultant in his unsuccessful first attempt at running for the office of mayor of New York; subsequently, Giuliani officiated at Ailes's wedding and brought him gifts when he was hospitalized in 1998, which reflected their very personal relationship (Koppelman and Renzas 2007).

Though Fox might be one of the most overt violators of fair and impartial news reporting, it is certainly not alone. Even if it is now

125

recognized as a more contentious argument, American news media has long been criticized as left-leaning in regard to the political spectrum. For example, publications such as the *New York Times* were often blamed for stacking their editorial boards and op-ed pages with liberal opinion writers, and, though subjective opinion is obviously allowed on those pages, the imbalance of the personnel at least gave the appearance of political bias. Other news organizations have also been accused of substantial political favoritism, such as CNN with its moniker the "Clinton News Network" because of its apparent favoring of Bill and Hillary Clinton (Kincaid 2007). We shall revisit these cases later and introduce others to further argue how they may qualify as instances of corruption as we will subsequently define it.

Understanding Corruption

Despite the broad and varying instances of corruption that have occurred in the world both recently and long in the past, most academic analyses of corruption refer to a narrow sample of institutional corruption, for example, political corruption like bribery (Noonan 1984; Pritchard 1998), while the most common recognition of corruption in academic literature is the abuse of public office for personal or private gain (Nye 1967). Though political corruption of various kinds is certainly paradigmatic of corruption, corruption is a much broader phenomenon.

In this chapter, we will argue that corruption is a pervasive form of immorality that exists in various social institutions, and as such its connection with mass media institutions such as journalism is twofold. First, one of the primary responsibilities of journalists is to report on matters of public interest, including revealing and reporting on corruption in society. In this way, journalism has a morally positive relationship with corruption because it exposes this concealed wrongdoing for the public's interest. Second, with the increasingly concentrated and politically aligned corporate media, journalism has in some instances itself become corrupt, leaving it with a second and morally negative relationship with corruption. Therefore, in this chapter we will attempt to achieve several broad goals, two of which are conceptually central. We will show how journalism is and can be an exemplary anti-corruption institution for society. However, we will also describe how journalism has itself, in some instances, been corrupt, in part because of its increasing vulnerability to corruption. We will also give a robust conceptual account of corruption from a neutral perspective, that is, a basic conceptual analysis of corruption per se.

Journalism and Corruption

One of the primary purposes of journalism – particularly investigative journalism – is to uncover concealed wrongdoing, including corruption, within various social institutions. However, for it to optimally uncover institutional corruption, journalism itself must be relatively free from corruption. For, as we hope to show, much of the corruption in journalism reduces its effectiveness in uncovering corruption both inside and outside of journalism.

Think of some famous instances of journalistic wrongdoing in the last 20 years of Western, and particularly American, journalism: Jayson Blair of the fabled *New York Times* fabricated dozens of quotes, interviews, and stories before his shameful resignation (Barry et al. 2003; see Chapter 1); Jack Kelley of *USA Today* fabricated stories and lifted quotes from other sources over 10 years as a senior reporter (Morrison 2004); John Laws, an Australian radio host, took payments from a consortium of banks in exchange for positive public commentary without disclosure of his financial arrangement with the banks (Johnson 2000; see Chapter 5). That financial arrangement saw the light and was made public only when investigated and exposed by *Media Watch*, a weekly investigative journalism program aired by the Australian Broadcasting Corporation (ABC); Janet Cooke fabricated a Pulitzer Prize-winning story about a fictional eight-year-old heroin addict that cost her her job and the prize, among many other consequences for the

Washington Post and its deceived readers (Ettema and Glasser 1998). Rupert Murdoch's News Corp. was accused of intentionally biasing news content and coverage choices (Greenwald 2004). The Federal Communications Commission in the United States and Australia's former prime minister John Howard independently lobbied for reducing restrictions on cross-media ownership in their respective jurisdictions despite its obvious degradation of journalistic quality and standards and its effect on corresponding democratic processes.

These are just a small sample of instances of journalistic wrongdoing among persons, organizations, and the industry that we will argue are not only unethical but also corrupt. Among several things we must explore, therefore, are (1) what distinguishes corruption from other forms of wrongdoing, and (2) what conditions inherent in the current institutional structure of journalism are conducive to corruption. To answer these questions, we need to know more about the institutional structure of journalism, and the conceptual essence of corruption.

What is Corruption?

To understand the phenomenon of corruption generally and in journalism specifically, we must first understand the concept of corruption – particularly institutional corruption via corrupt actions. To do so, we will follow the lead of recent scholarship in the field (Thompson 1995; Miller 2001; 2005, Miller et al. 2005). Instances of corruption vary substantially, exist in diverse phenomena and in different degrees of severity, but there are common ties between all forms of corruption. First, all forms of corruption are immoral, though not all forms of immorality constitute corruption. Moreover, many forms of corruption, such as political bribery, are illegal, though some, like fabricating stories in journalism, are not. As with relations between the law and morality generally, the class of corrupt and illegal acts, while often related, are distinct. For example, the law itself can be corrupt, such as it was in Nazi

Germany, in South Africa under apartheid, and as it is presently in Mugabe's Zimbabwe.

Moreover, corruption exists in at least two broad rubrics: non-institutional personal corruption and, our primary target in this chapter, institutional corruption (Thompson 1995; Miller 2005). Broadly speaking, non-institutional personal corruption exists in instances in which there is a despoiling of a person's moral character outside of the institutional domain. However, institutional corruption exists in at least three ways: in individual persons, in organizations, and across an entire industry.

It is useful to consider institutional corruption in terms of its necessary and sufficient conditions:

1. An instance of institutional corruption is an instance in which an action or set of actions undermines a legitimate institutional goal(s) or purpose(s) and/or despoils the character of an institutional role player (s). We call this the *institutional actor condition.*
2. To be corrupt, an action or set of actions must involve a corruptor who performs the action or a person who is corrupted by it. We call this the *person condition.*
3. An action or set of actions is corrupt only if it corrupts something or someone. We call this the *cause and effect condition.*
4. An action or set of actions is corrupt only if the person who performs it can foresee – or at the very least, could and should have foreseen it – and can reasonably avoid the action. We call this the *moral responsibility condition.*

A common trait of institutional corruption that is not, however, a *necessary* condition, is its predominantly *systemic* nature. As Miller (2005) argues, corrupt acts and/or corrupt institutional goals and purposes are a result of systemic immoral acts rather than one-off actions. In other words, a journalist who plagiarizes once, is caught, but never does it again has certainly committed an immoral act but not an act of corruption since it is highly unlikely to have despoiled one's character or to have undermined an institutional goal, such as causing a rash of plagiarism by other journalists. It is our view that corruption can occur from a single act – though quite rarely – but the magnitude of such an act must be of such epic proportions and its effects so deleterious that it satisfies the four necessary and sufficient conditions above.

Typically, the despoiling of character or institutional goals occurs after systemic immoral actions, such as frequent plagiarism or fabrication (see the argument on personal corruption and Jayson Blair below). However, we include this caveat because of the logical possibility that a massive act of immorality that is well publicized and has profound psychological effects on others may in fact constitute corruption. As an example outside of journalism, one may argue that the September 11 terrorist attacks single-handedly corrupted many Americans' (and non-Americans') views of Muslims. Many Americans associated Islam with terrorism to the point of acting violently against people who merely appeared to be of Arabic descent in the days and months following September 11, 2001. However, for a single action to constitute corruption, it took a massive (and rare) occurrence like this. Though there may or may not be a precedent for this in journalism, its possibility certainly exists.

Conditions conducive to corruption

Corruption, as described above, most often occurs when certain conditions exist that make it more likely to occur (Klitgaard 1988; Pope 2005). Corrupt politicians, for example, often accept bribes for monetary gain or some further form of power offered by someone who possesses an excess of wealth and/or power. Much of this activity escapes public scrutiny and punishment because of the lack of oversight by a governing agency or legitimate social watchdog. Because factors such as wealth and power recur in separate cases of corruption, it is useful in our analysis to identify an explicit set of conditions that are conducive to corruption and provide corruption's defining characteristics.

According to Spence (2005, 2009), the following conditions are conducive to corruption and are present in nearly all cases of corruption – power, opportunity, and disposition (2005, 4). There-fore one may have the power to corrupt but without the opportu-nity one's power would be insufficient to achieve a corrupt act. But even if one were to have the power and the opportunity, without possessing the disposition to act corruptly, one would usually lack the will to corrupt other persons or processes.

Part and parcel of these conditions are the primary characteristics of corruption: self-regarding gain, concealment, and the abuse of a fiduciary duty of trust (Spence 2005, 4). Therefore, corruptors typically corrupt persons or processes for personal or private gain, such as in the paradigm cases of bribery or fraud. Second, because corruption is often illegal and always immoral, most corruptors go out of their way to conceal their acts of corruption. Finally, corruption generally, and institutional corruption specifically, suc-ceeds in many instances because corruptors abuse pre-existing trust-based relationships; for example, police may succeed in var-ious forms of corruption because of the trust-based relationship they typically have with the members of the society they serve.

Instances of Corruption in Journalism

Similar conditions and characteristics of corruption can occur within journalism. To begin with, many social institutions are more easily corruptible because journalists often fail to present a serious threat as a legitimate watchdog of political, economic, and other forms of institutional corruption. Our argument here is that much of the inadequacy of journalism as watchdog stems from its financial and commercial alignment with advertisers and investors, its political alignment with corrupt politicians, and the increasing tendency for the concentration of ownership. We will say more about this towards the end of the chapter.

Furthermore, within the institution of journalism itself there are many conditions that are conducive to corruption, as evidenced by the recurring instances of corruption mentioned earlier in this chapter. The first condition is that it possesses enormous *power*.

Journalism can harness massive financial power, and possesses the power of public persuasiveness because of socially influential journalists and also because of its gate-keeping effect and its broad reach, among other factors. By the same token, journalists have the *opportunity* to use their power. Because the public relies on journalists to uphold its trust-based relationship within society, journalists frequently have the opportunity, while acting with impunity, to lie and mislead the public if it serves their interests. The third and final condition conducive to corruption, *disposition*, is also evident among journalists. Clearly, journalists such as Jayson Blair and Jack Kelley were disposed to corrupt actions as evidenced by their repeated, intentional actions. Repeated and apparently intentional immoral behavior typically indicates the corruption of one's disposition or character, which, in short, is one's basic habitual behavior either in one's life generally or in one's role (i.e., as journalist) specifically.

Closely related to these conditions are the common characteristics of corruption: self-regarding gain, concealment, and the abuse of a fiduciary duty of trust (Spence 2005). Among nearly all instances of corruption is the presence of self-regarding gain, whether to one's direct personal advantage or to the indirect advantage of one's friends or allies. Again, journalists like Jayson Blair and Jack Kelley fabricated news for personal advantage, while journalists who work for politically biased news organizations may corrupt news in part for the sake of, or out of loyalty to, their employer. Concealment is another common factor, for it allows corrupt journalists to engage in corruption with impunity and thus to avoid any reprimand for their legally or ethically objectionable actions. Once Jayson Blair was discovered fabricating news, for example, he was forced to resign from the *New York Times*. Finally, institutional corruption is also typically characterized by its breach of a fiduciary duty of trust, which in many cases is what provides concealment. For if members of the public trust journalists to perform according to the ethical conventions and commitments of their profession, this trust acts as a cloak that allows journalists to act with impunity.

Moreover, apart from the afore-mentioned conditions and characteristics of corruption, there are a number of sub-conditions and sub-characteristics that fit under the umbrella. It would be too onerous to mention them all, but we will discuss some examples given by Miller et al. (2005) in their recent book on corruption. Miller et al. point to the example of Colombia, where social institutions were fraught with difficulties stemming from a massive inequality in wealth, few shared moral norms, inadequate governance, an imbalance of power, and persistent conflict, most of which was a result of the drug lord Pablo Escobar's stranglehold on the illegal trade of cocaine (Miller et al. 2005, 30–32). Many of these conditions exist in journalism as well, though for different reasons.

First, when there are too *few shared moral norms*, journalists have no basis on which to act consistently with one another in practice. Though there is some consistency in the principles, values, and virtues in codes of ethics and other ethics literature and conventions, these principles, values, and virtues are often either misunderstood by journalists or ignored because of industry pressures. Therefore, this first sub-condition gives way to the second sub-condition in journalism that is conducive to corruption, that of *moral confusion*. While in many cases there is some general agreement among journalists about what values, principles, and virtues matter in journalism, there are widely ranging ways in which these values, virtues, and principles are understood, or for that matter, misunderstood. Moreover, ethics documents such as codes of ethics and codes of practice rarely give adequate descriptions about what their terminology means. For example, what is fairness? What are the ways in which we can understand truth or truthfulness, or balance, or integrity?

The third sub-condition conducive to corruption in journalism lies in the *conflicting goals and loyalties* of journalists, particularly high-ranking editors and news managers. For example, even the most moral executive editors of franchised newspapers are necessarily torn between their often conflicting duties of delivering the best possible news and maximizing profits. Although they must deliver high-quality objective news to meet their ideal obligations, they are also expected to appease shareholders and advertisers in ways that keep circulation high and advertising at a premium.

This brings us to a fourth sub-condition conducive to corruption in journalism, which, as in corrupt societies like Colombia for much of the 1980s and 1990s, stems from a gross *imbalance of power*. Journalism has struggled with its own form of power imbalance increasingly over the past 40 years, as ownership has shrunk from a wide base of independent owners to an entire nation's media being dominated by just a handful of owners. For example, in a study that measured the proportion of market control taken by the top five newspaper and TV companies in each of 12 countries, there was a marked trend towards intense concentration of ownership. "The top five newspapers account for an average of 66.7% of total circulation. Television markets are even more concentrated – on average the top five firms cover 89.5% of total viewing" (Djankov and McLeish et al. 2001). The Prime Minister of Italy, for example, Silvio Berlusconi, controls through his media organization, 80 percent of television channels in that country. This lack of ownership diversity can create a gross imbalance of power, which in many cases leads to severe consequences. One such consequence is that the content which qualifies as news under a powerful media regime can be carefully geared towards supporting or at least not challenging alliances with powerful political and economic interests or allies. The "news" is skewed to support those interests, as we will detail more towards the end of the chapter.

The fifth and final sub-condition conducive to corruption in journalism is a *lack of effective institutional oversight* in terms of self-governance or governance of any other kind. In journalism, particularly US journalism, this is an especially contentious issue because of the negative freedoms (freedom from interference) assigned to journalists vis-à-vis the right to free speech. Because the right to freedom of speech is so widely recognized and invoked in Western journalism as a trump card against legal and non-legal challenges to journalistic speech, perhaps nowhere more so than in the United States, it can often be used to block and obstruct legitimate efforts to reduce corruption in modern journalism. Therefore, when journalists fail to self-regulate in an effective, systematic, and consistent manner, they enjoy what may be an unparalleled lack of oversight and as a result largely avoid legitimate institutionally sanctioned consequences. Journalism may be one of the few social institutions in which there is no substantial legal or non-legal recourse against corruption.

A common abuse of such free speech rights in the United States occurs with libel and defamation. Free speech rights place such a strong burden of proof on the person or group claiming to be libeled or defamed that even proof of a false statement is not in itself considered sufficient evidence for a successful suit. That is, defamed public figures must convince a judge that the accused speaker intended actual malice against them. In essence, this relatively high degree of free speech is meant to ensure that members of the public – most often journalists – can criticize their government leaders without fear of unjust reprisal. But as happens in some cases, the strong implicit and explicit protections of free speech often invite corruption via negligence on the part of news media, particularly when it fails to govern itself adequately and commits unjustified forms of legal but immoral speech.

One of the more recent examples of contentious tests of free speech occurred in 2005 when a Danish newspaper and several other newpapers published cartoons depicting the prophet Muhammad as a terrorist, a proponent of violence, and an oppressor of women, among other criticisms. The rioting that ensued in several primarily Muslim nations caused the death of more than a dozen people, as well as the destruction of the American and several European embassies in Arab nations. There is strong reason to hold that the newspapers publishing cartoons like these bear a high degree of moral responsibility for the subsequent rioting and violence, because the rioting was both foreseeable and avoidable. Though the newspapers that published these cartoons, along with those who supported their publication, believe that the right to freedom of speech protects such speech acts, there ought to be a serious concern for preventing harm that some forms of speech can incite.

Moreover, though even potentially harmful speech must be protected in some instances, there must be strong and justifiable reasons for allowing it. In other words, where harm is likely to occur to people because of a speech act, we must consider if the speech act is still, all things considered, justified. For example, if there were riots in the streets in 1940s Germany against the Nazi party, we could say, with the wisdom of hindsight, that their harmful consequences would have been worthwhile had they succeeded in planting doubt about Nazism in the minds of the German public.

When we are dealing with moral conflict, such as when we attempt to compare the potential positive and negative consequences of a contentious speech act, we must therefore consider if there are overriding reasons to exercise that speech act – even when it is likely to cause someone or something harm. In the case of the Danish cartoons, no reasonable explanation was given for their publication other than a weak blanket reference to freedom of speech. This case seems therefore to satisfy the *institutional actor condition*, as it appears to be a fortuitous act of religious prejudice that in essence corrupted the legitimate institutional goals of journalism such as remaining objective, fair, and balanced. For the second condition, the *person condition*, it involved persons both as corruptors (the cartoonists) and corruptees (those who published the cartoons). For the third condition of corruption, the *cause and effect condition*, it was clear the cartoonists caused the corruption, which produced not only the effect of being published but also the negative consequences that followed, several deaths and severe damage to embassies from associated vandalism.

Finally, there appear to be several layers of moral responsibility for the corruption and its negative effects. First, there is the moral responsibility held by the cartoonists for creating the prejudiced cartoons, because arguably the rioting effect was to a reasonable person both foreseeable and avoidable. Second, there is the moral responsibility of the publishers for voluntarily publishing the cartoons, when a reasonable person would expect a violent reaction to them. Finally, the rioters themselves most definitely bear some moral responsibility. Though they did not provide the impetus for them, they were responsible for the riots, which resulted in the deaths of several people.

While political cartoons are meant to use images to convey opinions, they must still be used responsibly, for there must be a justifiable reason for publishing a cartoon that may cause offense. However, though such justifications do not admit of proof, it seems the cartoons were merely a shallow attempt to undermine the dignity of a religious group. The cartoons appear to have offended Muslims by questioning the legitimacy and purpose of Islam. They infuriated millions of Muslims who, given the current political and cultural tensions, are in many cases trying to reconcile their own beliefs with those of the Western world. Therefore, the harm that unjustified free speech can produce is tantamount to corruption which typically hides under a false veneer of a well-respected right: the right to deliver information that is in the public's interest – not effects that are clearly against the public interest.

Personal corruption

Perhaps the paradigm case of personal corruption in journalism in the new millennium is that of Jayson Blair (see Chapter 1 for further details), formerly a reporter for the *New York Times*. Over the course of about three years, Blair consistently fabricated news – often entire stories – while lying to his supervisors about his whereabouts, pretended to be on assignment in locations throughout the United States while remaining in New York City. During his short tenure with the *Times*, several sources cited in Blair's articles complained to the newspaper's management until, finally, the *Times* performed an audit on him. Several *Times* reporters researched for weeks and produced a massive article detailing Blair's extensive instances of deception, to which he later confessed (Barry et al. 2003). Let us now examine, step by step, why Blair's actions are corrupt.

His actions can be considered corrupt under the first condition of corruption – the *institutional actor condition* – because Blair, the corruptor, undermined several legitimate institutional processes, for example, by lying to his sources, lying to his audience, lying to his colleagues, among various other deceptive practices. Second, Blair satisfies the *person condition*, because he is a corruptor of legitimate professional goals and purposes, namely, he willingly and covertly lied and deceived for personal gain. Blair later claimed he was playing a game and enjoying his ability to successfully deceive such an enormously successful and proud company, the venerable *New York Times*. Though lying and deception can in rare cases be appropriate in journalism, they are acceptable means only when they are the *only* available means to legitimate ends, namely, serving the public's interest.

Blair's actions also satisfy the third condition for corruption – the *cause and effect condition* – because several people and organizations were affected by Blair's corrupt actions: Blair himself, several of his sources, his audience, and the *Times*. Blair himself may have become corrupted by his choice to undermine legitimate journalistic goals and purposes to the point where his immoral actions became habitual and part of his character. Therefore, his character was despoiled to the degree that he was no longer motivated to act as a good journalist would. Instead, he played self-serving games at the expense of all relevant corruptees, including perhaps himself.

Many of Blair's sources were also corrupted because he misused their words and contexts to fit his self-serving needs, fabricated words that they had not uttered, and lied to them about his purposes for requesting their information (Barry et al. 2003). Some sources reported their problems with Blair to the newspaper because of their concern for the immediate consequences of his actions, but also out of concern for their ongoing relationship with the *Times*, as some of them were frequent public commentators for the *Times*. Moreover, Blair's audience was corrupted by the mass of false information he reported over time, some of which was fabricated, and some of which was out of context. Therefore, audiences were deceived and as a result some people within that audience lost trust in Blair, the *Times*, and journalism generally, among other lesser and greater consequences.

The last and perhaps most significantly corrupted entity, was the *New York Times*. Blair damaged the *Times*' reputation and possibly its economic well-being. He also created rifts within the management. Some editors were willing to defend him against initial accusations because they believed his lies, while others insisted that he be fired. Ultimately, the managing editor Howell Raines resigned under pressure in the wake of the Blair scandal, despite his previous reputation for being a top editor.

Finally, Blair's actions meet the fourth necessary condition for corruption – the *moral responsibility condition* – because he was foreseeably and avoidably undermining legitimate institutional roles and purposes (Blair 2004). Though in many cases it would be difficult to determine a person's intentions, Blair claims that these corrupt actions were intentional in his 2004 memoirs, *Burning Down My Masters' House*, written just after his resignation. Therefore, Blair meets all four necessary conditions for *institutional personal corruption*. Moreover, there is at least one obvious condition in Blair's case that was conducive to corruption. It is possible, if not likely, that there were insufficient supervisory (oversight) measures in place at the *Times*. There is evidence for this not only in Blair's perpetual acts of corruption but also in that complaints from Blair's readers, sources, and subjects did not raise the alarm to which adept editors should have responded with an earlier audit. Because *Times* editors waited more than a year after the earliest complaints of Blair's inaccurate or deceptive work was made available to them, it showed substantial weaknesses in the newspaper's self-governance.

Organizational corruption

Organizational corruption also involves corrupt or corrupted persons, but the causal origin and/or effect of the corrupt action emanates from an organization – a group of persons united, ideally, by some similar legitimate goal. However, if the group is united by a similar illegitimate goal, this is one way in which an organization can be subject to corruption. For example, a news organization that has a policy – official or unofficial – of partisan political support to which its employees are expected to subscribe, is committed to a corrupt organizational policy, for such a policy corrupts the legitimate organizational role of journalism, which is to provide objective and unbiased reporting. Although individuals are involved in organizational corruption to some extent – for, clearly, people are the ones who have (intentionally or unintentionally) developed the policy, instituted it, and acted on it – much of what promulgates and makes the policy binding lies not in individual persons but in an immoral organizational culture. And some, many, or all of the organization's members are thus collectively responsible to varying degrees. Bad institutional cultures are thus another condition in the professions that can be conducive to corruption, in this case, organizational corruption.

In journalism, organizational corruption often manifests itself in the form of conflicts of interest because of special interests like political partisanship. Most journalistic conflicts of interest result from the clash between journalists, who in most cases aim at objective reporting, and executives of news organizations, who may compromise their editorial role for the sake of advertisers or political allies. Though it has long been a concern in journalism that the metaphorical wall between advertising staff and editorial staff ought never to fall – and that concern is still strong – political partisanship unofficially proffered by news organizations in the form of political bias, seems to have trumped concerns about special treatment of advertisers in modern journalism. This is primarily because of increased media concentration. The following cases are examples of complications resulting from media ownership concentration which we will examine in relation to corruption.

Sinclair Broadcasting Group and Fox News

Just weeks before the 2004 US presidential election, the Sinclair Broadcasting Group, which controls 62 television stations in the United States, announced its plan to air a prime-time news feature in which presidential candidate Senator John Kerry would be ridiculed for allegedly indirectly encouraging practices of torture against prisoners of war in Vietnam in the early 1970s. The filmmaker proposed that Kerry's postwar comments criticizing American troops for abusing innocent Vietnamese people sparked a renewed interest in torture against American prisoners of war in Vietnam. Conversely, Kerry supporters said the film was a propaganda tool filled with false claims and loose causal relations to the violence, namely, that Kerry's anti-war stance caused the torture of American POWs.

Notwithstanding the validity of the torture accusation, the timing of the broadcast of *Stolen Honor* – slated to be anywhere from two weeks to four days before the presidential election depending on location – was potentially disastrous for Kerry in light of the closeness of the race according to pre-election polls (virtually a dead heat as of October 17, 2004). This case at least implies a strong political bias in favor of Bush by Sinclair. Sinclair's decision was so contentious that the company decided to fire its Washington, DC bureau chief after he publicly voiced his dissent over the decision to air the program because of its clear political bias. Jon Lieberman, the fired journalist, called the film "biased political propaganda, with clear intentions to sway the election" (Folkenflik 2004, 1). It was also noted that Sinclair was one of George W. Bush's most significant campaign donors (Sydney Morning Herald 2004).

The Sinclair case is similar in many ways to the relationship between Rudolph Giuliani and Fox News described at the beginning of this chapter. Because of the political favoritism shown by Fox News to the Republican presidential nominee, Giuliani stood to benefit unfairly from politically partisan coverage cultivated by years of previous professional and personal relationships between Giuliani and key Fox News executives.

As we can see, both Sinclair's firing of Lieberman and Fox's partisan coverage of Giuliani are demonstrations of organizational corruption – corruption of the processes of objective, impartial, and fair journalism. If there were adequate editorial independence, Sinclair would have taken on board Lieberman's objection by changing its broadcasting schedule in the Washington, DC area. Lieberman had requested it and ought to have had the influence to bring it about. But editorial control at Sinclair originates from non-editorial management staff, and in a way that undermines journalistic protocol.

In instances of organizational corruption it is often difficult to determine who or what group is responsible for causing corruption. In some instances, it may be a single person who enforces corrupt policy, or it may be a matter of slow and morally corrosive habits that worsen over time and take hold of unsuspecting practitioners. Nevertheless, in journalism and many other institutions, organizational corruption is similar to personal corruption, except that the cause of corruption is an official or unofficial organizational policy or decision.

In the cases of Sinclair and Fox, the organizations satisfy the first necessary condition of corruption because they undermined the legitimate institutional process of providing impartial, objective news in the public's interest. That is, some institutional actor(s) instantiated a policy, official or unofficial, that led to the undermining of legitimate journalistic goals. Though not all broadcasted information must be impartial because not all of it is news, all editorial or news documentary footage falls within the purview of content that ought to be objective.

Furthermore, there is the matter of broadcasting politically biased content close to an election. The notion of equal apportionment of airtime is based upon the moral presupposition that (1) in fairness all politicians ought to have an equal right to the amount of time allotted for political mass-communicated messages, and (2) politicized commentary dressed as objective news is an injustice to both the targeted candidate and the affected voters.

Sinclair and Fox News also satisfy the second necessary condition of corruption – the person condition: there is a corruptor (Sinclair/ Fox) and/or a corruptee (John Kerry, voters, etc.). Though we cannot determine precisely what person or group of people is directly responsible for the act in question, it was clearly an administrative decision coming from a representative or representatives of Sinclair and Fox respectively.

Sinclair and Fox satisfy the third necessary condition for professional corruption – the cause and effect condition – because it had a corrupting effect on something – both the journalistic and political processes – and someone – John Kerry and his campaign, Giuliani's Republican competitors, and finally voters who were subjected to or affected by the relevant broadcasts. The fourth and final condition is the most contestable because it requires a determination as to whether Sinclair and Fox acted in a way that could have foreseen or avoided a corrupting effect on the electoral process, the journalistic process, or both.

Some anecdotal evidence supports the view that Sinclair and Fox foreseeably and avoidably committed a corrupt act. Sinclair's Washington, DC bureau chief, who was later fired for his outburst, claimed that it was intentional partisan propaganda by Sinclair managers (Sydney Morning Herald 2004). Moreover, Sinclair is purported to be a major donor to the Bush re-election campaign (Sydney Morning Herald 2004). Though it cannot be established with absolute certainly that Sinclair acted corruptly in this case, the limited evidence available suggests that it is a strong possibility. The Giuliani corruption claim we make is supported by Giuliani's strong personal ties with Fox executives. There is, at the very least, the potential for a conflict of interests in Fox's coverage of Giuliani because of the basic difficulty of friends maintaining impartiality in dealings with one another. Because journalism requires impartiality, this potential conflict of interest should, at the very least, raise red flags for Fox audiences and Giuliani competitors.

In conclusion, organizational corruption has much in common with personal corruption because its basic elements – the corruption of legitimate institutional processes or purposes or the despoiling of the character of role players – are the same. However, the instigation for organizational corruption usually comes from a collective of persons who lead or are part of an organization. Though there are a range of ways in which organizational corruption manifests itself in journalism, most organizational corruption seems motivated by special interests, such as economic or political concerns as in the cases discussed above.

Industrial corruption

Finally, there is industrial corruption, which involves a particular industry supporting a corrupt practice which undermines one or several of its legitimate institutional roles or purposes. Two potential causes of industrial corruption in journalism are media concentration and media conglomeration. While there is no conclusive evidence to prove that either trend directly causes corruption in all organizations that it affects, there is strong evidence to show that concentrated and conglomerated media are more prone to corruption than non-concentrated and non-conglomerated media because of their inherent vulnerabilities, such as concentration of power.

Media concentration reduces the overall number of media owners, who as a consequence have greater media power because they hold an increased proportion of the market. If the views of media owners are imposed on news content, they undermine the legitimate institutional role of providing impartial and objective information. Although concentrated media ownership does not necessarily lead to an imposition of company views, it does, however, at the very least reduce the diversity of news judgments by limiting the overall number of editorial "visions" among owners, executives, or their legitimate editorial role players, who are of course journalists. Kovach and Rosenstiel (2003) describe the phenomenon: "This shift [towards further deregulation] could reduce the independence of the news media and the ability of citizens to take part in public debate."

Media concentration and conglomeration which could have been controlled by media companies themselves by refusing to aggregate more media organizations is partly responsible for the drastic decrease in diversity of news organizations which, many have claimed, has degraded much of Western journalism (Herman and Chomsky 1988; Bagdikian 2000; Kovach and Rosenstiel 2003). In the early 1980s about 50 corporations dominated Western mass media, but by the late 1980s the number had shrunk to under 30. By 1997, 10 firms dominated international mass media (Bagdikian 2000). A lack of diversity leads to a narrower range of editorial views if corporate executives affect editorial decision-making. Given the evidence above concerning News Corp. and Sinclair, this seems to be the case in at least some instances.

However, most instances of industrial corruption are enabled by laws that at one time restricted concentration and conglomeration in various industries with monopolies or near monopolies becoming a factor. Rockefeller's Standard Oil Trust in the United States in the late 1880s is a paradigm of how the monopolization of goods is bad for nearly everyone except the owner of the monopoly because it eliminates the marketplace competition without which fair prices for the consumer cannot be protected. Therefore much of the blame for industrial corruption in journalism falls on those who have promoted further concentration and conglomeration in the past 10 to 15 years, or have failed to oppose further concentration and conglomeration, such as the Federal Communications Commission of the late 1990s to the present.

Moreover, conglomeration opens up new opportunities for conflicts of interest because companies no longer focus exclusively on specific news platforms like newspapers, radio, or television, nor for that matter do they own only news media; in many cases, conglomerates, like Viacom, own news organizations, media entertainment companies, book publishing companies, and amusement parks, among other business entities that often compete against one another for reinvestment opportunities. That is, the better a particular business is at making profits, the higher a priority it may have within the conglomerate and the more money and resources it will receive to fulfill its goal for greater profits.

Moreover, there is room for intra-conglomerational conflicts of interest. Hypothetically speaking, would an investigative report on safety problems at a Viacom amusement park by a Viacom newspaper be trustworthy? Though it would clearly be in the public interest to investigate such a matter impartially, it is difficult to imagine a company publicly criticizing itself. In another example, imagine if Viacom could increase its overall profit by, say, increasing employment or company reinvestment in its theater operation, but at the same time reducing its staff or reinvestment in journalism as a counter-measure. Its multiple interests may thus conflict with its journalistic purposes and if so, this would deny journalism its requisite independence and possibly prevent the journalism

145

company from meeting its moral goals. In a big business with multiple interests, there is seemingly little motivation for companies to behave in ways that support journalism when journalism is not its most profitable branch. Nevertheless, there are other, mostly legal, means which can override a company's corporate habits via regulation.

Media ownership regulation

Media ownership regulations exist in various forms and for the purpose of maintaining a certain standard of quality among various media, including journalism organizations. Much of the regulators' time consists in balancing ownership laws with economic potential to create an acceptable if not ideal journalism industry. However, many nations – including the United States and Australia – have become increasingly laissez-faire about media ownership restrictions, allowing a greater proportion of overall market share per owner both within certain media and across media. Big business and government in these countries support the anti-regulation attitudes for the sake of economic growth. But many civic organizations and even individual journalists want greater regulation for the sake of sufficient news diversity and autonomy (both individual and organizational), which typically leads to a better quality of journalism.

In the United States in 2003, the Federal Communications Commission attempted to further deregulate media ownership, though it was stymied by the US Court of Appeals. The FCC proposed loosening regulations that would have allowed US television networks such as Fox (News Corp.) to buy several more television stations nationally, and result in one company owning the biggest newspaper and highest-rated television station in almost any given city (Ahrens 2005). The FCC panel's majority defended its move to deregulate by claiming that the Internet has relieved the public of any concerns relating to news diversity, because, it claims, people have greater access to more information than ever before. Furthermore, the FCC commissioned studies

(Brown and Williams 2002; Levy et al. 2002; Roberts et al. 2002; Williams and Roberts 2002; Williams et al. 2002; Woldfogel 2002; Cunningham and Alexander 2004) which support the notion that deregulation is best for the public interest for the following reasons:

1. There is a sufficient variety of opinions presented to the public.
2. There is sufficient coverage of news and public affairs.
3. There is a sufficient variety of programming available to the public.
4. There is sufficient coverage of local issues.
5. Individuals and organizations have sufficient access via advertising to present their views to a larger audience.

However, criticism of this view has come from many sides. For example, one member of the five-person panel of the 2005 FCC, Democrat Jonathan Adelstein, claims he has strongly opposed the majority Republican commission's push for media deregulation. Adelstein, consistent with proponents of increased regulation, claims that further FCC deregulation would harm small communities because of a decrease in local news. "I want to make sure that what we do serves the public interest and not the interest of corporations that seek to profit" (Patch 2005). Even the US Federal Court of Appeals, which rejected the FCC's move for deregulation, complained these claims were made on the basis of "irrational assumptions and inconsistencies" (Baker 2002).

A critique of the FCC's proposed move towards deregulation, sponsored by the American Federation of Television and Radio Artists, the Newspaper Guild-Communication Workers of America, and Writers Guild of America East, concluded that deregulation

does pose a problem in maintaining a diverse flow of entertainment and information for individuals as well as reasonably priced advertising options for businesses ... it is reasonable to believe that media outlets would be reluctant to air news or entertainment that reflected badly on either the media company itself or a major advertiser. (Baker 2002)

Like many possible cases of corruption, it is difficult to conclude that the FCC and/or the 10 major media outlets that have interests in deregulation are in fact corrupt. However, FCC members are appointed by the White House, which means that the majority of FCC members' political affiliations usually shift to match the President's political party. It is no mystery that George W. Bush had pro-business agendas and that it is likely that his highly politicized FCC appointees supported his agendas; moreover, the FCC chairman during the 2003 deregulation push was a Republican, Michael Powell, son of Colin Powell, who was President Bush's Secretary of State in his first term as president.

Determining an act of industrial corruption, like all cases of corruption, requires four necessary conditions as detailed above: (1) a corrupt action is one that undermines legitimate institutional processes or goals or despoils the character of an institutional role player; (2) a corrupt action must involve a corruptor who performs the action or a person who is corrupted by it; (3) an action is corrupt only if it has a corrupting effect, that is, it corrupts something or someone; and (4) an action is corrupt only if the person who performs can foresee and avoid it, or could and should have foreseen and avoided it.

If we consider that the purpose of journalism organizations within media companies is to serve the public in matters of public interest, then a company's choice to undermine that goal for the sake of profit is a matter of organizational corruption because each organization is acting on its own behalf. However, if the FCC, which exists to regulate the industry for the sake of, and on behalf of, the public's interests, but works instead in the interests of partisan politics, then it too undermines legitimate institutional processes of both journalism and politics. On that basis it would seem that it also stands guilty of industrial corruption, since its actions affect (corrupt) the entire industry.

Therefore, the first necessary condition of corruption – the institutional actor condition – is met in cases in which a legitimate institutional goal or purpose is undermined – the goal of both politics and journalism to serve the public's interest in their respectively relevant ways. The second necessary condition of corruption – the person condition – is met because both the FCC and the media ownership collective were potential corruptors – they mutually pushed for media deregulation, which in effect undermines legitimate institutional purposes and goals by making journalistic organizations editorially non-autonomous. The third necessary condition for corruption – the cause and effect condition – is met because there is a corrupting effect on journalism's ability to deliver diverse information to the public and the public's ability to use diverse information in various civic matters, like voting. The fourth and final necessary condition for corruption – the moral responsibility condition – may or may not be met, though, as the criticism of the FCC cited above claims,: "it is reasonable to believe that media outlets would be reluctant to air news or entertainment that reflected badly on either the media company itself or a major advertiser" (Baker 2002).

Conclusion

Our aims in this chapter have been to explore several facets of corruption in the media: first, we provided an examination of the concept of corruption, through which we offered a conceptual framework of corruption. After modifying the concept of corruption, we developed the following model.

1. An instance of corruption is an instance in which an action or set of actions undermines a legitimate institutional goal(s) or purpose(s) and/or it despoils the character of an institutional role player(s).
2. To be corrupt, an action or set of actions must involve a corruptor who performs the action or a person who is corrupted by it.
3. An action or set of actions is corrupt only if it corrupts something or someone.
4. An action or set of actions is corrupt only if the person who performs it can foresee – or at the very least, could and should have foreseen – and can avoid the action.

We then distinguished between different forms of corruption: institutional corruption from non-institutional corruption, individual corruption from organizational corruption and from industrial corruption. Each of these categories, though similar, has separate origins and separate effects. Therefore, any effort to develop an anti-corruption method requires that the idiosyncrasies of each form of corruption be understood.

Finally, we provided examples of how corruption manifests itself in the persons, organizations, and industry of journalism. From this conceptual analysis, we have drawn several conclusions. First, there are instances of personal corruption among journalists. Former journalists such as Jayson Blair and Jack Kelley have admitted their corrupt actions. Second, there are several likely instances of organizational and industrial corruption. For example, material evidence and suspect habits imply that Sinclair Broadcasting Group and News Corp. are likely to have some corrupt organizational policies or tendencies. Third, the institutional structure of journalism for persons, organizations, and the industry make journalism vulnerable to corruption. Moreover, regulatory bodies like the FCC, if corrupt, can affect the ability of the entire industry to meet its goals.

Chapter study questions

1. In most cases, is it likely that a single action will constitute corruption or is corruption more likely to be systemic? Name one case in which a single action can be perceived as constituting corruption.
2. The Jayson Blair case, as argued in this chapter, constitutes a case of personal institutional corruption, but might it also extend to organizational and/or industrial corruption? If it does, give reasons why and describe how.
3. Describe what is meant by despoiling one's character.
4. List as many legitimate institutional goals in journalism as you can imagine. How are those goals morally justified? Select two of these goals and describe how they can be undermined by (a) personal corruption and (b) institutional corruption.

5. Describe a common instance in journalism that makes the fourth necessary condition of corruption – the moral responsibility condition – difficult to uphold in respect of one being able to foresee an instance of corruption but have great difficulty avoiding it.

References

Ahrens, F. (2005) FCC drops bid to relax media rules. *Washington Post*, Jan. 28, A1.

Bagdikian, B. (2000) *The Media Monopoly*, 6th edn. Boston: Beacon Press.

Baker, D. (2002) *Democracy Unhinged: A Critique of the FCC Studies on Media Ownership*. Washington, DC: Department for Professional Employees, AFL-CIO.

Barry, D., Barstow, D., Glater, J., et al. (2003) Correcting the record. *New York Times*, May 11, A1.

Blair, J. (2004) *Burning Down My Masters' House: My Life at the New York Times*. New York: New Millennium Audio.

Brown, K., and Williams, G. (2002) *Consolidation and Advertising Prices in Local Radio Markets*. Washington, DC: Federal Communications Commission.

Buettner, R. (2007) In Fox News, Giuliani finds a friendly stage. *New York Times*, Aug. 2. http://www.nytimes.com/2007/08/02/us/politics/02FOX.html, accessed Dec. 10, 2009.

Cunningham, B., and Alexander P. (2002) A theory of broadcast media concentration and commercial advertising. *Journal of Public Economic Theory*, 4, 557–575.

Djankov, S., and McLeish, C., et al. (2001) Who owns the media? Harvard Institute of Economic Research, Apr. 2001, discussion paper 1919. http://post.economics.harvard.edu/hier/2001papers/HIER1919.pdf, accessed Feb. 5, 2006.

Ettema, J. S., and Glasser, T. (1998) *Custodians of Conscience*. New York: Columbia University Press.

Folkenflick, D. (2004) Sinclair fires D.C. chief who spoke out. *Baltimore Sun*, Oct. 19. http://articles.baltimoresun.com/2004-10-19/news/0410190049_1_jon-leiberman-sinclair-broadcast-group-hyman, accessed Apr. 14, 2006.

Greenwald, R. (2004) *Outfoxed: Rupert Murdoch's War on Journalism* (video documentary). Disinformation Company.

Herman, E. S., and Chomsky, N. (1988) *Manufacturing Consent*. New York: Pantheon Books.

Johnson, R. (2000) *Cash for Comment: The Seduction of Journo Culture*. Annandale, NSW: Pluto Press.

Kincaid, C. (2007) Still the Clinton News Network. *Accuracy in MediaI*, Jan. 8. http://www.aim.org/media-monitor/still-the-clinton-news-network/, accessed Nov. 13, 2009.

Klitgaard, R. (1988) *Controlling Corruption*. Los Angeles: University of California Press.

Koppelman, A., and Renzas, E. (2007) Rudy Giuiliani's ties to Fox. *Salon*, Nov. 16. http://www.salon.com/entertainment/video_dog/current_tv/2007/11/16/alex3/index.html, accessed Nov. 8, 2010.

Kovach, B., and Rosenstiel, T. (2003) All News Media Inc. *New York Times*, Jan. 7. http://www.nytimes.com/2003/01/07/opinion/all-news-media-inc.html, accessed June 17, 2007.

Levy, J. M., Levine, F., and Levine, A. (2002) *Broadcast Television: Survivor in a Sea of Competition*. Washington, DC: Federal Communications Commission.

Miller, S. (2001) *Social Action: A Teleological Account*. New York: Cambridge University Press.

Miller, S. (2005) Corruption. In Edward N. Zalta (ed.), *Stanford Encyclopedia of Philosophy*. http://plato.stanford.edu/entries/corruption/, accessed Oct. 2, 2009.

Miller, S., Roberts, P., and Spence, E. (2005) *Corruption and Anti-Corruption: An Applied Philosophical Approach*. Upper Saddle River, NJ: Prentice Hall.

Morrison, B. (2004) Ex-*USA Today* reporter faked major stories. *USA Today*, Mar. 19. http://www.usatoday.com/news/2004-03-18-2004-03-18_kelleymain_x.htm, accessed Nov. 8, 2010.

Noonan, J. T. (1984) *Bribes*. New York: Macmillan.

Nye, J. (1967) Corruption and political development: a cost–benefit analysis. *American Political Science Review*, 61(2), 417–427.

Patch, J. (2005) FCC official warns against media consolidation. *Des Moines Register*, Oct. 6. http://www.desmoinesregister.com/apps/pbcs.dll/article?AID=/20051006/, accessed Dec. 17, 2006.

Pope, J. (ed.) (1997) *National Integrity Systems: The TI Source Book*. Berlin: Transparency International.

Pritchard, M. S. (1998) Bribery: the concept. *Science and Engineering Ethics,* 4(3), 281–286.

Roberts, S., Frenette, J., and Stearns, D. (2002) *A Comparison of Media Outlets and Owners for Ten Selected Markets: 1960, 1980, 2000.* Washington, DC: Federal Communications Commission.

Spence, E. (2005) Corruption in the media. In Jeanette Kennett (ed.), *Contemporary Issues in Governance: Proceedings of the GovNet Annual Conference.* Melbourne: Monash University.

Spence, E. (2009) Corruption in the Media. *International Journal of Applied Philosophy,* 22(2) (Fall 2008) 231–241.

Sydney Morning Herald (2004) Anti-Kerry film sparks row. *Sydney Morning Herald,* Oct. 20. http://www.smh.com.au/articles/2004/10/19/1097951701643.html, accessed Apr. 14, 2006.

Thompson, D. (1995) *Ethics in Congress: From Individual to Institutional Corruption.* Washington, DC: Brookings Institute.

Williams, G., and Roberts S. (2002) *Radio Industry Review 2002: Trends in Ownership, Format, and Finance.* Washington, DC: Federal Communications Commission.

Williams, G., Brown, K., and Alexander, P. (2002) *Radio Market Structure and Music Diversity.* Washington, DC: Federal Communications Commission.

Woldfogel, J. (2002) *Consumer Substitution among the Media.* Washington, DC: Federal Communications Commission.

7

Two Dimensions of Photo Manipulation: Correction and Corruption

Trauma and Drama

News photographers strive to capture traumatic and dramatic moments in many of the stories they cover.[1] Traumatic and dramatic pictures inform the public, create social awareness, and provide photographers with a sense of professional accomplishment. In 2003 *Charlotte Observer* photographer Patrick Schneider won a North Carolina Press Photographers Association award for traumatic and dramatic pictures he captured while, among other things, covering wildfires that ravaged parts of his home state and cost the lives of several firefighters. Schneider's pictures captured the intensity of wildfire fighting and the tragedy of human loss. However, the award was rescinded when it was discovered that Schneider had substantially manipulated his winning photographs by using a dodge and burn tool in Adobe's Photoshop imaging software to increase the

Media, Markets, and Morals, First Edition. Edward H. Spence, Andrew Alexandra, Aaron Quinn, and Anne Dunn.
© 2011 Edward H. Spence, Andrew Alexandra, Aaron Quinn, and Anne Dunn. Published 2011 by Blackwell Publishing Ltd.

traumatic and dramatic aspects of the pictures (Irby 2003). Though trauma and drama are often valuable photographic traits, they are not good or valuable in themselves – in order to be valuable to the goals of journalism, traumatic and dramatic images must convey the world truthfully by representing it accurately and objectively – these are fundamental aspects of *universal public morality*. The question, then, is whether Schneider undermined these key journalistic goals of objectivity and accuracy, and in doing so, threatened to corrupt the photojournalistic process.

This book has raised questions about many facets of morality in the media. One particular facet of unethical behavior – corruption – has been a central concern and one that has been discussed at length in Chapter 6. We take up issues with corruption again in this chapter but specifically with regard to the practice of photojournalism. As an increasing number of media – particularly news media – are shifting from traditional formats such as newspapers and magazines into web-based forums, there has been a decrease in the number of words and an increase in the volume and importance of images as modes of transmitting information. Therefore it is imperative for the public interest that media audiences generally, and news audiences specifically, trust the images they see. One of several reasons for the decline of public trust in news media is due to confusion about photographic integrity (Lester 1999; Irby 2003).

Particularly since the age of digital photography and digital editing, media critics have cast doubt on whether the images they see in print news are accurate and honest reflections of reality. Almost two decades ago *New York Times* photography critic Andy Grundberg predicted a tenuous prospect for documentary photography in the digital age: "In the future, readers of newspapers and magazines will probably view news pictures more as illustrations[2] than as reportage, since they can no longer distinguish between a genuine image and one that has been manipulated" (Grundberg 1990). At a 2007 National Press Photographers Association meeting in Portland, Oregon, Grundberg's nearly two-decade-old concern was reaffirmed. "Editorial control is being lost," John Long, NPPA's president, said. "The problems we're having now are not just ethical violations by photojournalists. Now there are editors, designers, and others who are altering pictures. Photographers who alter photos get fired. But we're seeing editors and others who alter pictures, and there are no repercussions" (Winslow 2007). By determining appropriate photo manipulation standards, part of which is determining how much journalists ought to rely on high-tech manipulations, we will establish guidelines that, if adopted, should hopefully rejuvenate public trust in digital images and improve journalism's public standing in general.

There are three broad questions to be answered in this chapter regarding photo manipulation and ethics: (1) What are the proper ethical guidelines for post-shoot photo manipulations (manipulations made after the photo has been taken)? (2) Are photo manipulations unethical? (3) Furthermore, do photo manipulations constitute corruption of the photojournalistic process? Corruption in professions generally, and in journalism specifically, deserves attention because of its often pervasive and destructive nature. Since we aim to explore whether the manipulation of a photographic image – insofar as the manipulation causes an intentional or foreseeable inaccuracy – is an instance of corruption, we will rely on the outline of journalistic corruption in the previous chapter as a guide for evaluating photojournalism.

Making Choices

Before a news photographer lifts the camera to her eye she has the obligation to make choices – what lens to use, what camera settings to best match the available light, how close or far to stand from a subject so as to determine where the borders of the photo will be in terms of composition, among other considerations. By at least one definition, each of these choices, put into action, is a form of manipulation (Elliott and Lester 2003).

There is also the form of manipulation that is part of the photo-editing process. This can be a benign matter of color correction or a problematic form of manipulation that compromises accuracy for the sake of aesthetics. While many of these manipulations occur during the photo shoot for the sake of adapting to changing lighting conditions, in most cases they occur on desktop computers in the newsroom with the aim of improving aesthetic appeal.[3]

Here we plan to analyze key instances of photo manipulation by borrowing from two key areas of philosophy: epistemology and ethics. In this argument the two will be strongly intertwined. One example occurs in our discussion of reality. Since one moral premise of news reporting is that one ought to report objectively – that is, to report objective or at least impartial information – it is imperative that photojournalists follow suit by recording and publishing only realistic images insofar as they are objective or impartial. Realistic images are those that are captured, processed, and published using methods that convey images that correspond as closely as possible to the way things exist in the world. In this discussion we suggest this is what those methods ought to be.

Of course "oughts" imply normative analysis and this is where we give way to moral theories. For the purpose of this chapter we will employ an ethical analysis that borrows from several ethical doctrines, including consequentialism, deontology, and virtue theory, all of which will help us evaluate the journalistic issue. We also hope that this ethical examination, both theoretical and practical, may be of help to photojournalists and news audiences in enabling them to better understand the issues surrounding image manipulation that guide them in meeting their individual as well as their collective moral and practical ends.

For example, utilitarianism, a form of consequentialism, can be viewed as an effective ethical guide to the practice of photo manipulation in cases when maximizing aggregate news value can be seen as a morally good and hence desirable end. One manner in which this can be done practically is to maximize instances of journalistic truthfulness,[4] for without truthfulness, journalism is without moral grounding and credibility (Merrill 1997). One way we can maximize truthfulness in the news is by promoting photojournalistic standards that require photographic integrity.

However, there may be instances in which a deontological moral approach better embraces what is morally good. As we saw in Chapter 2, deontology offers a notion of morality derived from the inherent rightness of a principle applied in action. In other words, actions are chosen because they are considered to have inherent moral worth, not because of a goal of or a perceived result from the action.

Finally, we will add virtue theory to strengthen the deontological and consequentialist arguments in terms of their motivational aspects. Although deontology and consequentialism offer strong and coherent decision-making procedures, virtue theory offers a framework through which analysts can pinpoint the specific virtues and values that are most relevant to a given moral issue. Therefore virtues like truth-telling and integrity offer complementary motivational force to the formal decision-making procedures of consequentialism and deontology.

Categories of Image Manipulation

Manipulations occur at several phases in the photographic process: before the shoot, during the shoot, and after the shoot. Pre-shoot manipulations are usually the most blatant, as they involve issues such as posing subjects, which, while it may be acceptable in advertising and public relations photography, is under most circumstances ethically unacceptable in news photography because of the expectation of journalistic objectivity, which precludes at the very least most active forms of reality alteration except in an occasional instance for feature photos. Since our focus here is on documentary news photography, we shall avoid analyzing pre-shoot manipulation, canvass the issues faced during photo shoots, and focus most on the more nuanced aspects of post-shoot manipulation during digital editing.

Post-shoot conduct is the most commonly explored aspect of photo manipulation because it presents the greatest technical challenges and the majority of the moral problems that arise in digital imaging.

Although unethical manipulation started with darkroom photography, and is more than a century old, the need for further exploration is evident because of the continuing decline in public trust in the media, which is in part related to poor photojournalistic practice (Tompkins 2002). Many scholars and journalists believe that digital manipulation practices, both morally positive and negative, increased with new technology, because high-tech tools make manipulation more expeditious (Lowrey 1998). Therefore, we shall now describe the moral values and virtues that are crucial to guiding ethical practice in photojournalism.

Journalism Values and Virtues

In order to make ethical determinations we must first refer to sound moral reasoning. Within journalism, professional codes and rules of conduct have long been available but are in some cases poorly conveyed, and often unenforced. Therefore, developing coherent and explicit professional standards and implementing them are an important start in creating an ethical environment in news photography. Because the newsgathering processes of photojournalists and text reporters are so similar in terms of their *telos* – serving of the public interest – they share the same foundational set of values. These are essentially journalistic virtues, as they all have qualities that closely correspond to traditional epistemological virtues such as truthfulness, accuracy, honesty, completeness, independence, credibility, and balance amongst others – values that are essential for guiding and supporting morally defensible behavior (Cocking and Oakley 2001).

These core journalistic values are essential to journalistic practice because they are conducive to objective reporting and truth-telling. (We review the term "truth" as it regards photojournalism in the following section.) Without an attempt by the photojournalist to be impartial with regard to the news, the visual newsgathering process becomes tainted with unknown bias and prejudice, which are symptoms of journalistic vice.

Credibility is an important value in relation to photo manipulation and is closely related to (or generated by) the virtue of honesty. Essentially, credibility is most at risk when readers realize they have been deceived by a photo, become skeptical and ultimately lose faith in the photojournalistic process. This skepticism can not only result in the loss of readers, which is bad for the press in terms of economic sustenance, but more importantly, it can motivate individuals to forsake journalism as a news source, therefore lose a vital tool in an informed citizenry.

Accuracy, which corresponds closely to the traditional virtue of truthfulness, is also a seminal journalism value in regard to photo manipulation. Since the goal of the photojournalist, aside from obvious technical limitations, is to recreate reality, she has to be as accurate as possible in terms of technical considerations (composition, light, shadows) and as free as is humanly possible of ideological influences (imposition of personal and political biases on news events). But whenever we mention accuracy, as it relates to photojournalism, we never mean to imply exact reality. What is meant rather is an effort towards precision, conceding only to insurmountable technical and physical limitations such as the loss of a physical dimension – that is, the shift from the three-dimensional world to a two-dimensional representation (newspapers, computer screens, etc.).

Manipulation, as we have seen, takes more than one form – not all manipulation is bad; nevertheless, some is. Manipulation that is morally problematic is manipulation that changes an image's veracity and potentially results in deception or misunderstanding. This is not to imply there is less (or no) truth-value in artistic or drastically manipulated images, rather that journalism is the wrong forum for artistic, manipulated photographs in most cases. The primary reason for this is functional. By analogy, consider whether newspapers that use poetry as their dominant style would be as effective in portraying public interest information as the objective reporting method currently used. Although this question is rhetorical, and poetry is certainly an effective style for some sorts of expression, we must realize that each style fits a particular function, and news uses objective reporting to portray matters in the public interest. Let us now see what a prominent code of ethics says about manipulation.

According to the professional code of the National Press Photographers Association in the United States, "editing should maintain the integrity of the photographic images' content and context. Do not manipulate images or add or alter sound in any way that can mislead viewers or misrepresent subjects" (NPPA 2004). As we can see, there is nothing in the language of this or most other codes that is ethically controversial. It is in the interpretation of this statement that problems may arise. One of the aims of this chapter is to provide an unambiguous interpretation of the above statement and others like it, in terms of a clear conceptual analysis of what constitutes manipulation in photojournalism that is deceptive and misleading and therefore ethically objectionable and possibly corrupt.

What is Real?

Although photographic images portray only a fraction of a given news event, it is the duty of the photographer to treat all aspects of that slice within justifiable journalistic and moral constraints. Although choices related to news judgment are essential to conducting oneself during a photo shoot, it is not part of this analysis per se because it deserves separate attention for its unique array of complexities.

Since we have already determined the inherent flaws in recreating reality, we must now acknowledge that journalistic reality is a matter of verisimilitude. A mortal enemy of closeness in photojournalism is the self-regarding desire some photojournalists have for inauthentic beauty. Aesthetic desires beget complex moral considerations in photojournalism because practitioners often fight internally for or against artificial beautification, which challenges the truth-telling advantages of accurate but potentially less beautiful photographs. Moreover, it is beautification performed with public impunity that constitutes corruption. But we will say more about that shortly.

In this chapter we will define *reality* very broadly as whatever exists in the world independently of our wishes, beliefs, opinions, judgments, or statements about it. We may wish that we could take to the air and fly unaided just by flapping our arms, but that wish does not correspond with reality. The law of gravity and the laws of aerodynamics of this world frustrate any such wish regardless of how vigorously this wish is felt or expressed. In keeping with our proposed definition of reality, we will define *truth* as the semantic relationship between our beliefs, opinions, judgments, or statements on the one hand, and reality on the other.

According to this *correspondence definition of truth* – a notion of truth dating back at least to the ancient Greek philosophers – true beliefs, opinions, judgments, or statements are those that correspond to reality, correspond to how the world is independently of those beliefs, opinions, judgments, or statements. It is the reality of the world that makes our beliefs, opinions, judgments, and statements true and not our beliefs, opinions, judgments, or statements that make the world real. Our reality check is to ensure that our statements, oral or visual, describe or depict reality truthfully, and they do so when the words or images used to make those descriptions correspond with how the world actually is in reality and not how we wish or imagine it to be.

According to our correspondence definition of truth, a photograph is *true* if it corresponds to reality as closely as it is reasonable to expect, given the visual transformation from a three-dimensional world to a two-dimensional image. Analogously, a photograph is *untrue* if it deviates from its correspondence to reality in the ways in which a two-dimensional image is capable of representing reality. This philosophical inquiry about realism and truth necessitates two further distinctions about photographic accuracy: pictorial accuracy and epistemic accuracy. We define the two concepts as follows. *Pictorial accuracy* concerns the relationship between a photographic image reproduced in a publication and what was in the photographer's visual field at the moment the image was captured.

Epistemic accuracy, on the other hand, concerns the meaning garnered from the photographic image by the audience of a journalistic publication in which the image is displayed.

Although a photograph in isolation may *depict* reality accurately it may nevertheless fail to epistemically *describe* reality accurately. This could be because the image, though pictorially accurate, is somehow contextually atypical. For a simple example, imagine a photograph of someone who has jumped a few feet in the air with the length of their body parallel to the ground, It could appear that the person is free falling from a great height if there is nothing but sky in the background and no ground in the frame of the image. Though the image is pictorially accurate in respect to what is in the visual field, it could be misunderstood because there is no frame of reference in respect to the subject's distance from the ground.

As basic and important as pictorial accuracy is, epistemic accuracy is no less important as the above example demonstrates. For an otherwise accurate depiction of a photographic image could still be rendered deceptive or at least confusing through a false, misleading, or atypical context. Therefore, although pictorial accuracy is certainly necessary for ensuring the integrity of photographic images reproduced in journalistic publications, it is not sufficient to preclude an appropriate understanding of the truth. For that reason, although photojournalists will be deemed ultimately responsible for the pictorial accuracy of their photographs, editors and other journalists will be deemed ultimately responsible for the selection of the contexts in which they place otherwise pictorially accurate photographic images.

Although photojournalists are primarily responsible for pictorial accuracy, those photojournalists who knowingly or foreseeably allow their photographs to be placed in a misleading context likely to deceive viewers are also morally responsible for the epistemic accuracy of their photographs. Therefore, a photograph will be deemed unethical or immoral if its untruth has a tendency to deceive or mislead its intended audience, either by (1) design or (2) negligence through pictorial or epistemic inaccuracy or both. The immorality of an untrue photograph will be deemed to be directly proportional to the relevance that the truth of the photograph has to its visual semantic content. Hence the immorality of an untrue photograph will vary directly according to the capacity of its semantic content to deceive.

Many photojournalists think it is harmless to make minor touch-ups for visual aesthetics so long as they don't go "too far." But, for example, when photographs with overcast skies are infused with yellow and orange hues in Photoshop for the sake of increasing aesthetic appeal the photo becomes morally tainted. The color change alters the image from its more accurate form. As North Carolina Press Photographers Association's President Chuck Liddy said in regard to a recent photojournalistic scandal (see above), "As news photographers, we have a duty to accurately portray what we see, not what we *want* to see" (Irby 2003).

The issue of reality came to the forefront in 2003 when *Los Angeles Times* photojournalist Brian Walski was fired after it was discovered that he had combined two of his Iraq combat photos to make them appear as a single original picture. Walski had what he described as "the best day I had in a string of good shooting days in Iraq" (Johnston 2003). Walski's altered photograph ran on numerous front and inside pages in national newspapers before a *Hartford Courant* employee noticed something indicative of unethical manipulation – several Iraqis crouching in the background of the image appeared twice. The *Courant* contacted the *Times'* picture editor, which prompted apologies to readers for the manipulation in several newspapers that had published the photo, as well as Walski's firing from the *Times*.

Walski, who was contacted by satellite phone the day after he submitted the photos to the *Times,* admitted to the fabrication and regretted his choice. "After a long and difficult day, I put my altered image ahead of the integrity of the newspaper and the integrity of my craft," he later told the *American Journalism Review.* "These other photographers are there [in Iraq] risking their lives and I've just tarnished their reputation" (Johnston 2003). Fortunately, such bold and reckless forms of manipulation are rare. Kenny Irby, visual journalism group leader at the Poynter Institute, called Walski's decision "unprecedented" (Johnston 2003). However, there are numerous milder forms of manipulation that occur regularly in news photography, many of which lack clear ethical guidelines in respect to codes of ethics or journalistic convention. In the next section, we will examine several of the most common forms of news photo manipulation and try to make those guidelines clearer.

Common Practices

Below is a list of commonly accepted manipulation practices, some of which many argue are routine and innocuous. Based on afore-mentioned moral theories, an argument will be made for accepting or refuting each practice or at least some manifestation of it.

Color balance

Color balance requires a photographer to render a match (or the closest thing to a match) of the colors in an image to those of the scene photographed. Color balance commonly involves consistently correcting technical flaws (acceptable) and making aesthetic improvements (unacceptable).

In their photographic renderings of color many digital cameras range from imperfect to heavily flawed. No matter what camera lighting settings are used for the various basic lighting scenarios (daylight, outdoor cloudy, fluorescent, incandescent, tungsten, etc.), images often appear with color casts that can range from mild to severe. This is one situation in which Adobe Photoshop digital imaging software – the industry standard – is a savior. It allows for color corrections that enable an image to convey as close a realization of realism as possible.

On the flip side, this function can be easily abused. For example, it is not uncommon for photographers to "warm" or "cool" photographs as an added effect after making a legitimate color correction. Warming involves artificially infusing reds, yellows, or a combination thereof for aesthetic reasons, which is analogous to someone wearing make-up – which may make them possibly prettier, but is unnatural. Cooling involves artificially infusing shades of blue, and is popular for cold weather photos or for enhancing already existing colors, although in most cases irresponsibly. The mere act of color correction often tempts photographers to make aesthetic enhancements that go beyond acceptable adjustments used to recreate reality, therefore violating the virtues of accuracy and integrity.

To avoid this problem photojournalists have the option of abandoning color manipulation altogether and simply accepting what the camera offers. The advantage to such a choice is that the photojournalist stays beyond reproach in respect to unethical aesthetic changes. However, most photojournalists would argue that there are exceptions that would make such an absolutist approach untenable – that there are enough flaws in the way cameras judge and record light that human judgment must in some cases override these flaws.

This is a scenario that at first sight seems to create conflict between two of the leading doctrines of moral philosophy. Immanuel Kant, the deontologist, might say: "No, one must not manipulate photographic images under any circumstances because manipulation may result in deception and deception being inherently morally wrong is in all circumstances ethically objectionable." A utilitarian like John Stuart Mill might on the other hand say: "Yes, the overall maximization of utility (say, happiness) depends upon people being informed by way of relatively accurate, if not perfect, portrayals of color. These results are more important than the harm that might result from the occasional misjudgment or abuse." It is our view that until camera technology advances to a stage in which there are far fewer photographic flaws, Mill's approach trumps Kant's because the photographer or editor, correctly motivated to produce accurate pictures, will make fewer errors.

Cropping

Cropping is the process of eliminating elected outer edges of an image to increase the impact of the item or subject that is thereafter displayed more prominently in the image. Use the full frame as much as possible. If there were no risk in shooting pictures with the intention of cropping, then photographers would shoot all of their images "loose" and set their cameras to record large, high-resolution files and then crop to their hearts' delight. Modern technology allows for this: massive image files can be shot, from which small fractions are cropped, and the cropped image can then be enlarged while maintaining remarkable clarity.

Because of problems that can develop from cropping, photographers are trusted to use their judgment on how to compose a newsworthy photograph rather than worry about later alterations. But the reason for avoiding cropping is not as clear-cut as the color correction argument. For example, a photographer could argue that cropping a picture has no negative consequences since he could have legitimately made the same "tight" image by further zooming his telephoto lens or by moving closer to the subject. The problem with cropping, however, typically comes in two ways: unintended loss of newsworthy information and the much more problematic issue of presenting a subject in a misleading manner.

In the first instance photographers don't always remember the reasons why they shot a particular frame the way they did when they are editing many hours or days later. But almost no photographer would ever say he did not shoot a frame with a specific purpose in mind. Therefore, there is often reason to believe there is relevant visual data in an image that a photographer might overlook and eliminate in the cropping process. Great care must therefore be taken before a crop is made to avoid the potential loss of important information.

Photographers who crop might intentionally or unintentionally mislead an audience by removing photographic information. Gary Condit, the congressman who was a suspect in the disappearance and murder of his former intern with whom he was suspected of having an affair, Chandra Levy, was portrayed in what he thought was a misleading manner in a cropped photograph (Jacobsen 2001). The *NBC* photograph originally showed Condit with Levy under one arm and another woman, Jennifer Baker, under the other. The cropped photograph, however, removed Baker, leaving only Levy and Condit. Baker, who criticized the cropped picture, thought the picture was intentionally cropped to support the rumor of an affair between Levy and Condit (Jacobsen 2001).

Whether intentional or unintentional, the information loss is morally regrettable because it may cause confusion about the meaning of the image. If it is an intentionally deceiving crop, however, it may constitute an act of corruption because deception clearly undermines journalism's institutional goals of accuracy and objectivity and the negative consequences of the deception are both foreseeable and avoidable. A photo suggesting an unconfirmed affair, when it in fact provides no relevant evidence (even if the affair had occurred), clearly violates the photograph's moral goal of accuracy, and if it were presented this way intentionally, constitutes an act of corruption.

Despite cases like these, the option to crop photographs should remain available to photojournalists, but not without a certain awareness of the risk of losing photographic integrity. Cropping is valuable because it can make photographs more meaningful by increasing the impact of the image's salient regions. But ethical cropping is contingent upon maintaining photographic integrity. Careful cropping, then, will enhance the virtues of accuracy and integrity when its potential for enhancing meaning can be safely realized.

Responsible cropping is not a threat to the integrity of photographs, as long as it satisfies both conditions for acceptable manipulation mentioned above: (1) it must make the photo more accurate or meaningful and (2) it must be formulaic if it relates to the recreation of objective data. Since the first condition is satisfied in that the crop helps to increase semantic meaning, and the second condition is satisfied because the subjective decision taken to crop does not undermine objectivity though undermining truth or accuracy, cropping usually passes the acceptable manipulation test.

Dodge and burn

Dodge and burn techniques involve using imaging tools to brighten or darken selected parts of a photograph. Deceptive photographic manipulation can be likened to deception in speech. However, since digital technology has its own form of communication, which is initiated by keystrokes and mouse clicks, it requires a separate semantic representation. With photographs, the analogous process of "stating" is publishing with the intent of someone seeing a photograph. Essentially, the act of manipulating a photo can be likened to a speaker who would manipulate a phrase in her mind before speaking. Therefore, the published photo can be analogous to speech in that regard.

Dodging and burning can be used to make accurate micro tonal corrections (adjusting brightness and darkness) as compared to the macro tonal adjustments made using Photoshop tools such as "levels" and "curves" which change a range of tones in the whole photograph instead of a select region. Much like color correction, an ethically acceptable tonal adjustment hinges on an accurate representation of reality. Dodging and burning, like color manipulation, can go too far, such as when context and meaning are changed by drastically changing tonal detail.

Essentially, the photographer uses this manipulation technique to give artificial prominence to a subject, or a particular section of the photograph, although a common justification for the alteration is that it will help an audience better understand an image – that is, its aim is epistemic accuracy. Therefore, we have established a form of deception – the photojournalist knows the image is not pictorially genuine either by the intention of making an aesthetic improvement, or by attempting to assist in understanding by highlighting detail, or simply in the doomed but well-intended attempt to correct perceived imperfections. All but the latter are obvious forms of deception and even the latter is a form of deception, even if it is intended for helpful purposes.

As mentioned in the opening of this chapter, *Charlotte Observer* photographer Patrick Schneider was called to account for photographs he dodged and burned, three of which helped him win a North Carolina Press Photographers Association award, which was later rescinded because of the manipulations. Two photographs came from coverage of North Carolina wildfires in 2003 – one was an action photo of firefighting while the other was coverage of the funeral of a firefighter who had died fighting the blazes. The third picture was part of a photo essay on farming. Each of the three photographs had portions that were excessively darkened by a Photoshop burn tool to add inauthentic drama to the scenes. After the award was rescinded and Schneider was suspended by the *Observer* for three days, he admitted to having dodged and burned but defended his choices by citing the lack of clear standards about the use of dodge and burn (Irby 2003).

The main issue here is what manipulations constitute image correction and which constitute corruption. Photographers must understand that any steps beyond recreating reality, such as infusing drama into a picture through darkening it, is a corruption of the legitimate institutional goal of providing pictorially accurate images. To enable one to form the reasonable belief (a belief that any reasonable person would be epistemologically entitled to form) that photojournalists intend to deceive, one only needs to combine (1) the aforementioned statements, with (2) the fact that photojournalists know or ought to know that readers expect or ought to expect truth, accuracy, and reality to be present in any information communicated to them by journalists whether in the form of words or of photographic images (for the epistemological and ethical commitments to which information gives rise, see Chapter 2), and finally with (3) the fact that their audience are receiving something from a photojournalist that a photojournalist knows or ought to know to be otherwise than intended, whatever his intentions. This awareness of inaccuracy, therefore, arguably qualifies as intent to deceive.

Even if the known inaccuracy is viewed by the photojournalist as merely potentially misleading and tolerated on the basis of a calculated risk, such known inaccuracy could still be assumed to be an intention to deceive. Although this is a secondary notion of intent – meaning that the photographers' primary intentions are not necessarily to deceive – there are few, if any, photojournalists or photo editors who don't know (or if they don't know they ought at least to know) that their actions are likely to deceive, at least some of the time by default because of the inherent risk associated with this type of manipulation (Irby 2003). Therefore, although this second notion of intent may not constitute a robust intention to deceive readers, it nevertheless qualifies as intent because of the photojournalist's knowledge that false information that could have been prevented will reach its intended audience.

After incurring a suspension for dodge and burn manipulations in 2003, Schneider lost his job with the *Observer* in 2006 after another image of a firefighter was called into question for excessive color manipulation. Schneider's editor at the *Observer*, Rick Thames, said the picture "depicted a Charlotte firefighter on a ladder, silhouetted by the light of the early morning sun. In the original photo, the sky in the photo was brownish-gray. Enhanced with photo-editing software, the sky became a deep red and the sun took on a more distinct halo. The *Observer's* photo policy states: `No colors will be altered from the original scene photographed'" (Winslow 2006).

Conclusion

On the surface, the main concern with photo manipulation is that it sometimes distorts reality, or the closest version of reality a photograph can capture and convey. Although there are a number of abstract arguments about the definition of reality, insofar as photography is concerned, reality means capturing a still image that has as many accurate properties in color, lighting, shadows, and depth as a two-dimensional image allows with a reliable degree of consistency. Although it is a foregone conclusion that reality in photos is technically limited, a close rendering is desired because it is (1) presumed to be practical in what people need from the news, and (2) what people expect to find in a news source, because that is how they measure the credibility of that source.

Although the first point is self-evident, the second may need some clarification. Journalists' credibility leads to public trust, which is a hallmark of journalism because, without it, news loses its value. And journalists set these expectations by establishing certain virtues and other guiding principles, which include a trust protocol contingent on consistent execution of ethical actions, among other things, following codes of ethics. Although journalism values are not perfect, they are, for now, the best guide towards truth and reality that journalists can follow in their respective formats – radio, television, the Web, and newspapers.

There are obviously a variety of ethical constructs that can justify actions of different kinds. Sometimes they conflict, but regardless of their occasional clashes, they lend a form of ethical continuity to an agency that chooses to employ one or several of them. The purpose of this analysis is not to advertise a specific ethical doctrine but to show how these doctrines and the various ethical theories they support can be used to determine defensible moral behavior. So, going back to the imperfect practice of photojournalism, how do we increase the likelihood of producing an accurate, newsworthy image? The answer is: with consistency and reliability. This is accomplished by reducing the most confounding factor in photojournalism: self-regarding measures – the temptation for a photographer to artificially improve aesthetics. This can be aided by adopting a set of rigorous standards, such as those we offer in this chapter, which are used as a guide and enforced by practitioners.

But this analysis goes beyond even the surface concern of recreating reality. Preserving photojournalistic standards is largely for the purpose of rejuvenating and maintaining press credibility for the long-term sake of, among other things, protecting and improving democracy. Although the practical limitations these suggestions impose may seem restrictive, or at least inconvenient, they are necessary. Not only will they reduce human error, regardless of the photographer's intentions, but they will also protect the veracity and merit of journalism, which should be high on any practitioner's list of professional desires.

Yet another reason to greatly limit digital alteration and reduce public mistrust is that even the appearance of regular improper ethical action forces the public to mistrust the press.[5] However abstract this idea may seem, its effects are exacerbated by photojournalism's self-made reputation for ethical inconsistency. Because of either the ambiguity of manipulation standards or the consciously unethical nature of some photojournalists' standards, the public is skeptical of manipulation even when it is justifiable in the strictest sense. Public skepticism is sometimes so great that even good decisions are often assumed to be deceitful.

By developing a more consistent formula for ethical manipulation and eliminating error-prone practices – however rigid it might seem – we have a formula that can bolster public trust with only minimal impositions on practitioners. The formula we suggest is composed of two broad statements. First, photojournalists must retain their ability to make news judgments, that is, they must use their skill and judgment to choose what to photograph and when and where to photograph it. Second, photographers must minimize the alterations for measurements of tone, color, cropping, etc., so that the only changes that are made increase accuracy, even at the expense of aesthetics.

These rules are likely not only to make photojournalists more objectively consistent, but also to give the public evidence that photojournalists care about the veracity of their profession.[6] These new rules, coupled with a consistent, transparent manipulation policy within the profession, could be a tonic for healthier journalism and a more robust democracy. And insofar as deceptive photo manipulation constitutes corruption as described above, the implementation of such an ethical regime in photojournalism will reduce the risk of corruption. This is important, especially with regard to investigative journalism, for if the watchdogs themselves become corrupt, who will we trust to expose corruption?

Chapter study questions

1. Though Brian Walski's case of combining two photos to make one image is a clear case of pictorial deception, does it constitute corruption? Why?
2. Is using a dodge or burn tool in Photoshop ever ethically sound? If so, what conditions would make dodging or burning acceptable?

3. Correcting color is a routine part of image editing, so why was Patrick Schneider fired for the 2006 firefighter image in which he manipulated the color?
4. Was the severity of Schneider's punishment in 2006 appropriate?
5. Is the greatest loss in each of the cases mentioned above a lack of accuracy or is it the credibility lost by photojournalists, through the publicizing of their manipulations?

Notes

1. Most of the text of this chapter has appeared previously in A. Quinn and E. Spence, "Two Dimensions of Photo Manipulation: Correction and Corruption," *Australian Journal of Professional and Applied Ethics*, 9 (1) (2007).
2. Illustrations are, by definition, significantly altered photographs or drawings that are credited as such in journalistic publications so as not to mislead readers or viewers about the reality or origin of the content.
3. Two definitions of manipulation were chosen from the *Oxford English Dictionary*: (1) "To move, arrange, operate, or control by the hands or by mechanical means, especially in a skilful manner." (2) "To influence or manage shrewdly or deviously; to tamper with or falsify for personal gain."
4. Truth in journalism is often known as "journalistic truth" because the information journalists provide is intended to be bits of truth about something, because it is usually impossible to get the "whole truth" (Merrill 1997, 105–108).
5. Dennis Thompson (1995) developed the idea that even the appearance of conflicts of interest matters in politics because appearances often have the same impact on people as actual conflicts of interest. In this chapter, the same underlying idea is used as it relates to possibility/ expectation of photo manipulation. It is the underlying skepticism of both politics and photojournalism that sets the stage for this elemental mistrust from which the expectations come.
6. Newspapers regularly include in their pages policies that exist or change when controversy over their policies become public, such as in the case of Walski or Schneider. It would be beneficial for

newspapers that adopt new rules – such as these – to publicize them for the sake of making the public aware of the increased reliability of their photographs.

References

Cocking, D., and Oakley, J. (2001) *Virtue Ethics and Professional Roles.* Cambridge: Cambridge University Press.

Elliot, Deni, and Lester, Paul (2003) Manipulation: a word we love to hate. *News Photographer,* Aug.

Grundberg, A. (1990) Ask it no questions: the camera can lie. *New York Times,* Aug. 12, sec. 2, p. 1.

Irby, Kenny (2003) A photojournalistic confession. *Poynter Online,* Aug. 22. http://www.poynter.org/content/content_view.asp?id=45119, accessed Aug. 8, 2003.

Jacobsen, Aileen (2001) Faking it. *Newsday,* July 11, sec. B, p. 6.

Johnston, Cheryl (2003) Digital deception. *American Journalism Review,* May. http://www.ajr.org/article_printable.asp?id=2975, accessed June 7, 2009.

Lester, Paul M. (1999) *Photojournalism: An Ethical Approach.* Hillsdale, NJ: Lawrence Erlbaum.

Lowrey, W. (1998) Photo Manipulation in the 1920s and 1990s. Paper presented to AEJMC conference and published in AEJMC online journal, Oct.

Merrill, John (1997) *Journalism Ethics.* New York: St. Martin's Press.

National Press Photographers Association (2004) NPPA Code of Ethics. http://www.nppa.org/professional_development/business_practices/ethics.html, accessed Nov. 10, 2010.

Thompson, Dennis F. (1995) *Ethics in Congress: From Individual to Institutional Corruption.* Washington, DC: Brookings Institution Press.

Tompkins, A. (2002) Sliding sounds, altered images. *Poynter Online,* June 28, 2002. http://www.poynter.org/content/content_view.asp?id=3380, accessed Nov. 19, 2003.

Winslow, Donald R. (2006) A question of truth: photojournalism and visual ethics. *National Press Photographers Association,* Aug. 2. http://www.nppa.org/news_and_events/news/2006/08/ethics.html, accessed June 4, 2009.

Winslow, Donald R. (2007) Photojournalism ethics: the problem seems to be a lot deeper. *News Photographer Magazine,* June 1. http://www.nppa.org/news_and_events/news/2007/06/ethics01.html, accessed May 15, 2009.

Further reading

Bok, Sissela (1989) *Lying: Moral Choice in Public and Private Life.* New York: Random House.
Miller, S., Roberts, P., and Spence, E. (2005) *Corruption and Anti-Corruption: An Applied Philosophical Approach.* Upper Saddle River, NJ: Prentice Hall.
Spence, E. (2005) *Corruption in the Media.* In Jeanette Kennett (ed.), *Contemporary Issues in Governance: Proceedings of the GovNet Annual Conference,* Melbourne: Monash University.
Stille, Alexander (2001) Prospecting for truth in the ore of memory. *New York Times,* Mar. 10, sec. B9.

8

Promoting, Codifying, and Regulating Ethics

Introduction

Up to this point we have focused on understanding what the role morality of the media is, and pointing to some of the ways in which individual media practitioners as well as media organizations have failed to live up to that morality. In this chapter we consider how to help media practitioners understand and act in conformity with that morality. Broadly speaking, we are looking at the regulation of behavior. Regulation means not simply laying down and enforcing rules of behavior, but putting in place mechanisms which will make it more likely that people will, and can, act as they should. We look at the regulation of two areas – content and ownership – and consider a range of regulatory mechanisms. The fundamental importance of a free press makes regulation in both areas particularly problematic. Any attempt to enforce such regulation through, for example, government control may be seen as an illegitimate

Media, Markets, and Morals, First Edition. Edward H. Spence, Andrew Alexandra, Aaron Quinn, and Anne Dunn.
© 2011 Edward H. Spence, Andrew Alexandra, Aaron Quinn, and Anne Dunn. Published 2011 by Blackwell Publishing Ltd.

infringement of the freedom of the press. On the other hand, self-regulatory mechanisms can be seen as ineffective and self-serving. Moreover, lack of regulation of ownership may lead to concentration of ownership which itself may lead to loss of media diversity and independence.

Integrity Mechanisms

Most of our discussion in this book so far has concentrated on what might be called the *substance* of media ethics. We have looked, for example, at such general questions as the kinds of rights and obligations that media organizations or individual media professionals have, and the kinds of virtues media professionals should aim to develop. We have also looked at the application of general principles to particular cases. Of course, there is a good deal of controversy about the content of media ethics. But there is also a good deal of consensus. No one, for example, seriously claims that it is ethically acceptable for a newspaper reporter to simply fabricate stories about matters of real public interest, or for a newspaper to knowingly publish such stories.

However, questions of substance are not the only kinds of questions we need to address in trying to understand media ethics. Even if we are clear about how members of the media should behave, we are faced with the question of how to ensure that they actually do so behave – of how to *promote* ethical behavior. Note that even if we thought that all members of the media were morally decent people who wanted to do the right thing, it is likely that we would still need to promote ethical behavior, given the difference between the demands of ordinary morality and those of media ethics. Since what counts as doing the right thing is not always obvious in the case of media ethics, it will be necessary to assist members of the media to think about the issues they face and to reach agreement about how they should behave.

There is a wide range of tools which can be used to promote ethical behavior within an organization, industry, or occupation.

These include codes of ethics, complaints and disciplines procedures, licensing and registration procedures, professional education, as well as legal requirements. Collectively, we will refer to them as integrity mechanisms. We can distinguish two classes of such integrity mechanisms. The first are conduct-based – they establish, monitor, and enforce standards of conduct. Think, for example, of a professional complaints and discipline system which prohibits members of a profession from engaging in certain sorts of behavior, and imposes sanctions if they are found to have done so. The second class of integrity mechanisms is attitude-based. They function by developing and reinforcing cultural norms – the attitudes about appropriate behavior we internalize and use to judge ourselves and others. Though these two kinds of integrity mechanisms obviously influence each other, they are not identical. Consider so-called "ordinary morality," which applies to us in our day-to-day dealings with each other. While the law prohibits and sanctions really serious breaches of that morality, such as assault and robbery, much of our moral life is beyond the reach of the law. So the law does not (indeed cannot) mandate that we treat each other with kindness and consideration. Our concern to be kind, as well as our tendency to make harsh judgments about people who treat others unkindly, stems from our acceptance of a cultural moral norm. Cultural norms are important in professional ethics too. In particular the distinctive virtues of each professional group can be developed only where they are broadly practiced and valued: they cannot be regulated into existence. In fact, there are a variety of ways in which they are developed and reinforced: through education and publicity, prizes and awards, as well as through informal processes of organizational culture and personal moral leadership.

In considering the appropriate form of regulation for some area of activity, we face three kinds of interrelated questions: (1) *What* (if anything) should regulation try to achieve? What are the ends it is aiming at? (2) Assuming that there is reason to think that regulation is desirable, *how* it should try to achieve this? What means (what integrity mechanisms) should it use to reach the ends at which it is aiming? (3) *Who* should be involved in the formation and exercise of the favored integrity mechanisms? Much of this book is, of course, an attempt to provide an answer to the *what* question, concerning the aim of regulation, so we presuppose this discussion in most of this chapter, and turn now to the *how* and *who* questions. We should note, however, that a distinction is often drawn between what is called (somewhat misleadingly) regulation of content on the one hand, and regulation of ownership on the other. We return to questions specifically about the regulation of ownership later in the chapter. Here we focus on content, where this includes not simply the literal content of media output but also the means by which this content is gained.

Regulation of Content

As we discussed in Chapter 3, media organizations in Western societies are, at least to a large extent, commercial enterprises. As such they participate in the market and are constrained by market considerations. An important part of the role of the media is to service the demand for information and well-informed commentary. It seems likely that media organizations that do not demonstrate sufficient respect for the truth or objectivity will do worse in the market than those that do. At the same time, as we also saw in Chapter 3, there are good reasons to be wary of state regulation of the media. This is not to say, of course, that the media should be free of any legal restrictions. They will, for example, be forbidden from divulging the addresses of witnesses in serious criminal trials, or publishing state secrets. But such restrictions apply to everyone, for good reason: the media is not being singled out. (Similarly, supermarkets are forbidden from selling poison. This is not an attempt to restrain the trade of supermarkets, but an attempt to restrict access to poison.)

Perhaps, then, we should allow the media to be unregulated, letting market forces determine what is produced and disseminated by the media, and which media organizations survive and flourish. This would surely be better than having the state determine the content of the media and the structure of the industry. In fact, as the following schema indicates, there are a variety of intermediate regulatory positions between these two extremes.

Regulatory spectrum

Market factors	Targeted intervention	Self-regulation	Co-regulation	Explicit government regulation

"Targeted intervention" involves the state using its financial power to support certain market actors or activities as a way of helping to bring about outcomes it takes to be desirable. For example, the government may have a policy that it will purchase advertising only in media forums which meet certain standards. Perhaps, for example, media outlets which have been shown to consistently and willfully ignore basic demands of accuracy and fairness should be denied such revenue.

"Self-regulation" involves an organization, profession, or industry agreeing to abide by voluntarily adopted standards embodied, for example, in a code of conduct or code of ethics. In a true self-regulating system the relevant body (organization, etc.) has sole responsibility for regulating the conduct of its members. Neither the standards of conduct nor the sanctions imposed are legislatively underpinned, and the government does not directly intervene by monitoring behavior or applying sanctions.

Given the problems of government regulation of the media, the idea of media groups self-regulating is obviously attractive. However, there are difficulties of both practice and principle in media self-regulation. The first problem concerns the setting of standards which are supposed to apply to the media. Typically, this is done through the promulgation of codes of ethics for the industry, organization, or occupational group. These codes tend to be couched in general, aspirational terms. For example, Clause 2 of the Media, Entertainment and Arts Alliance (MEAA) code of ethics,[1] which is designed to guide the conduct of Australian journalists, advises that members

> Do not place unnecessary emphasis on personal characteristics, including race, ethnicity, nationality, gender, age, sexual orientation . . .

No rationale is offered for this advice. Presumably, it is meant, at least in part, to guard against reinforcing unfair negative stereotypes, and perhaps also to shield people in the news from having details of their private lives aired to satisfy the public's appetite for titillating information. Even if it is interpreted in this sort of way, it still remains extremely vague: what counts as *unnecessary* emphasis will, in many cases, be undetermined. No doubt the fact that the new CEO of a major corporation is a homosexual (or a fundamentalist Christian) is usually irrelevant to a report in the financial pages of his plans for the business. But what if the business is one that explicitly targets the "pink dollar," seeing homosexuals as a major market? Would mention of the CEO's sexual orientation or religious beliefs be unjustified in that case? Such vagueness means that often there are no clear, generally accepted expectations about standards of behavior.

Even where it is clear what the relevant standards are, there are real difficulties in responding to breaches of them. The pervasive problem here can be summed up in the idea that "self-regulation" actually means "self-indulgence." None of us are good judges in our own cause – we can usually find some reason why what looks, on the face of it, to be bad behavior, is really justifiable or at least excusable. There is no reason to think that occupational groups or enterprises are immune to this tendency, and indeed we have much historical evidence to the contrary.

This general problem takes on specific form at the level of industry, organization, or occupational group. Let us consider first occupational groups, representing journalists or other media practitioners, such as the Society of Professional Journalists in the United States and the Media Entertainment and Arts Alliance in Australia, which attempt to develop and maintain professional standards, through codes of ethics, codes of practice, and publicizing censurable acts. In most cases, these attempts seem to have had little impact. Apart from the problem of vagueness discussed above, there are at least two other salient reasons for their lack of effectiveness. First, membership of such bodies is voluntary, so they can have little control over the activities of non-members. Accordingly, the standards they set are not universally or even widely accepted by practitioners (Kiplinger 2005). Second, their power over their *own* members is very weak. While they have the right to censure or impose sanctions such as fines on their members, there is little incentive for members to remain if they disagree with the judgment passed on them or feel that the sanction is unduly harsh.

In a number of other areas, occupational groups are empowered to set and enforce standards across the whole occupation. Consider professions such as medicine or the law. Only those who have been recognized and accredited by their peers are allowed to call themselves doctors, for example, or to have access to certain venues for the practice of their craft, such as operating theaters. Consequently bodies such as medical registration boards, which are controlled, or at least dominated, by medical practitioners, have real power over those who wish to practice medicine: they must conform to the required standards or lose their livelihood. That power is delegated by the state. In terms of the regulatory spectrum depicted above, this is an example of "co-regulation" – the state delegates regulatory powers to occupational groups provided they meet certain conditions, such as developing and promulgating a code of ethics, establishing an effective complaints and discipline mechanism, requiring members to engage in ongoing professional education activities, and providing regular reports to a body that has oversight of these matters to demonstrate their effects in improving practice.

There is much to be said for co-regulation as a method for ensuring that occupational groups behave properly. On the one hand, with the requirement for the overseeing body to be shown that regulation is actually effective, co-regulation overcomes the problem of "self-indulgence" inherent in a system of pure self-regulation (discussed above). On the other hand, it leaves the design and implementation of the regulatory system to those who are best placed to understand the ethical issues faced by members of the occupation and the way in which regulation actually impacts on them.

Whatever the general advantages of co-regulation, however, it is unsuitable for the media. First, even though the state is at arm's length from direct intervention in the workings of the media in a co-regulated system, there must be real worries about the influence it can exert over the media occupational associations which would depend on the state for their power. Second, *any* system of restricting work in the media to those who have been approved by some licensing body, whether that body be a direct arm of the state, or empowered by the state, or gains such power in some other way, is contrary to the doctrine of freedom of speech and of the press. My right to free speech is not simply a right to be claimed against state attempts to prevent me from communicating with others – it is a right to be claimed against anyone who does so. Furthermore, there are good independent reasons to restrict practice in areas such as medicine and law to those who demonstrated their competence and integrity to their peers, given the highly specialized nature of competence in these areas and the damage that can be done by the incompetent or unscrupulous. Most media work, on the other hand, does not require anything like the same degree of specialized competence. While a sound training in journalism no doubt helps people become successful journalists, many of those who make valuable contributions to the media have no such training. Finally, given the wide availability and diversity of channels of communication, any attempt to limit media work to those who are approved by and who accept the judgment of a regulatory body can be successful only if such a body has enormous, and enormously intrusive, powers of surveillance and control.

We have pointed to problems inherent in attempts by media occupational associations to self-regulate. These problems largely stem from the lack of power of such associations over their members. A similar problem faces industry associations, which are dependent for their existence on the support and cooperation of their members. On the other hand, media organizations, such as newspapers, television stations, and the like, obviously do have power over their employees, so it is at least possible that they can set and enforce ethical standards for those who work for them. And many such organizations do have codes of ethics. However, in media organizations, especially commercial organizations, commercial considerations tend to make attempts at self-regulation either futile or superfluous. They are likely to be futile if the objectionable behavior (or the persons responsible for it) is nevertheless commercially worthwhile. They are likely to be superfluous if the organization has reason to dislike it anyway because, for example, it brings it into disrepute or offends an important part of its market.

We seem to have come to an impasse. On the one hand, external, especially state, regulation is problematic in that it conflicts with press freedom. On the other hand, self-regulation appears to be ineffective. However, notwithstanding the very real problems we have pointed to with both external regulation and self-regulation, there are reasons to believe that self-regulation, properly managed, can have positive effects on media ethics, without unduly compromising the freedom of the press.

There are a number of instances of self-regulatory schemes or devices which have been, to a greater or lesser extent, successful. For example, at the level of occupational associations, the Swiss Press Council is a voluntary association of journalists (who are not licensed), yet it has the power to censure journalists through publicity, and this is at least somewhat effective because it is widely respected by Swiss journalists (Bertrand 2000). The Swiss experience may not translate easily to less homogeneous and larger societies such as the USA or the UK. However, even in those societies occupational associations can play a role in improving the ethical behavior of their members. The activities of such associations, for example in promoting codes of ethics, can be one element in creating organizational cultures which develop and reinforce ethical behavior. Conditions for morally healthy organizational cultures include a managerial focus on ethics, a practice of rewarding ethical behavior, synthesizing consistent values among practitioners (Bowen 2004), and instituting a mechanism for ethical dialogue, particularly in newsroom disputes or in times of ethical confusion (Newton et al. 2004). Certainly a well-thought-through code of ethics, which has been developed through an ongoing process of discussion with practitioners, can play an important role in such a dialogue. In other words, while occupational associations do not have the power by themselves to produce an improvement in the behavior of their members, where there are other supportive structures in place, they can help to do just that. In the introduction to this chapter we pointed to two broad classes of integrity mechanisms, which we called conduct- and attitude-based. While the problems we have pointed to limit the effectiveness of conduct-based mechanisms, where codes of ethics and the like are understood to be attitude-based, they can have an impact.

Well-devised self-regulatory mechanisms – both conduct- and attitude-based – at the industry or organizational level can also do good. The fundamental difficulty inherent in self-regulation is that even when those involved in it genuinely want to behave well, and to have a regulatory framework that will assist them and others to do so, they possess within themselves two potentially incompatible motives. On the one hand they are concerned to develop meaningful standards and to enforce them in a dispassionate manner. On the other hand, if and when they actually do behave badly, they (usually) wish to be judged as leniently as possible for their wrongdoing. This problem of two competing motivations within a person has come to be known as the "Ulysses and the Sirens" problem. In *The Odyssey*, Homer tells us that on Ulysses' way home from the Trojan Wars he had to sail past the island home of the Sirens. The Sirens were women who sang so beautifully that any sailor who heard them was attracted towards them – and shipwrecked on the rocky coastline. Ulysses wanted both to hear the Sirens and not to be shipwrecked. He therefore stopped the ears of his crew with wax, so that they were unable to hear the Sirens' song, and had himself bound fast to the mast, with orders that no matter how he pleaded he should not be unbound until they were well past the island. Ulysses thus fulfilled his desire to hear the beautiful song of the Sirens, but because of his earlier precautions their song proved ineffective and he and his crew were not shipwrecked but managed to continue on their voyage.

Similarly, it is possible to structure self-regulatory devices so that the motivation to develop meaningful standards and to enforce them in a dispassionate manner remains effective, while the motivation to be judged as leniently as possible for wrong-doing is rendered ineffective, or at least less effective. Consider the workings of the Press Council of Australia, a body set up and funded by the newspaper and magazine industry in Australia to oversee its activities. Amongst other activities, the Council solicits and responds to complaints against its members. It does so by reference to a Statement of Principles, which is recognized in the codes of practice of individual publishers. That Statement was developed, in part, through an analysis of a survey of complaints received by the Press Council over a 10-year period, and with the help of the Council's majority of independent members (i.e., people who do not work in the industry). One indication of its effectiveness is that every critical adjudication made by the Council against a mainstream newspaper or magazine has been printed in the offending newspaper or magazine with due prominence (Australian Press Council 2008).

Of course, whatever the merits of the system put in place by the Press Council of Australia, it is arguably less than perfect. For example, it depends on members of the public making complaints, rather than having the capacity itself to detect and act on breaches. But to say that it is less than perfect is not to deny that it is at least to some extent effective.

We can see similar self-regulatory structures arising within individual media organizations. For example, there is a trend for news organizations such as the *New York Times* to employ ombudsmen (now often called "public editors"), who receive, investigate, and act on complaints about the accuracy and representativeness of the content of their publications, and who also have a role as an independent assessor of that content. The motivations for such appointments, at least in part, may have been to defuse criticism of these organizations in the face of scandals such as the revelation of Jayson Blair's history of fabricating stories, and Judith Miller's enforced resignation following claims that she had become, in effect, a stooge of the Bush administration, complicit in spreading falsehoods about such matters as Iraq's supposed weapons of mass destruction program. Nevertheless, they do seem to have provided an opportunity for the public to have their say, and to have contributed to a heightening of the discourse regarding journalistic professional standards.

Ombudsmen are well placed to promote ethical behavior and deter corruption. They have the advantage of onsite work in the newsroom environment they evaluate, have immediate access to news decision-makers, and, as (typically) well-credentialed journalists, they are familiar with the way newsrooms work and the pressures journalists face. Again, however, there are some obvious problems with the role of the ombudsman in a self-regulating organization. As employees of the organization that they are monitoring – dependent on it for job security, camaraderie, etc. – ombudsmen face an inherent conflict of interest because those who may face the strongest criticism – news editors and news managers – are also those with the power to hire and fire them. However, the appointment of journalists well known for their integrity, and the potential impact on the reputation of a media organization that dismisses an ombudsman for being overly critical, provide a degree of assurance that they will not become too cowed by the fear of management displeasure, and that management will tolerate at least a good deal of critical comment.

We have seen that the regulation of media ethics is particularly problematic given the need, on one hand, for a high degree of ethical probity and, on the other, for freedom from government interference. This makes self-regulation the most attractive, indeed perhaps the only, form of regulation suitable for promoting ethical behavior in the media. But as we have pointed out, there are problems inherent in the practice of self-regulation itself. Thus, for a system of media self-regulation to function properly, it must be constructed in ways that overcome or at least reduce such problems.

The impact of the Internet and the consequent rise of the "new media" raise interesting issues for the regulation of media ethics. The workability of the kinds of self-regulatory devices discussed here depends on the willing participation of members of the media, whether they be individuals or organizations. Some think that those working in new electronic media will increasingly do so without becoming employees of the currently dominant large media organizations.[2] If so, media workers are less likely to become part of the culture of such organizations, and less likely to identify themselves as members of a media profession, with consequent lessening of the influences which foster participation in self-regulation.

As of the date of writing, it is difficult to predict the long-term effects of the growth of the new media. There are, however, two salient facts which are relevant here. First, while there are now an enormous number of blogs, etc. which are not controlled by established media organizations, those organizations still dominate the dissemination of opinion and information, not just in traditional but also in the new media. The important point here is that media organizations play two functionally distinct roles: gathering and packaging information, and delivering it to consumers. While the development of the Internet means that anyone can now reach a potentially huge audience, the established media organizations still have a substantial advantage in their ability to gather information and put it into a form which consumers find attractive. Most of what happens in cyberspace, then, is not significantly different in terms of impact or implications than letter-writing, or the posting of public notices, even though it makes use of a different delivery mechanism. It does not fall into the sphere of media ethics in the sense in which we are using that term.

Second, the relatively small, but significant, number of electronic sites which clearly do count as media in our sense but are not owned or controlled by the large established media organizations, are themselves beginning to play a significant role in holding the established organizations to account. Consider the stunning fall from grace of the American TV news reporter Dan Rather (see Chapter 2). Rather presented a story on CBS TV which made allegations about President George W. Bush's youthful service in the Texas Air National Guard. Within minutes of the program finishing, speculation was being aired on media blogs that the documents Rather had relied on for the story were fake. Eventually, CBS investigated the allegations and concluded that the documents were indeed bogus, and Rather was forced out of his job shortly afterwards. Or consider a quite different sequence of events centering on the Australian Federal Election in 2007. A number of blogs[3] took issue with the way in which Australian newspapers made use of opinion polls during the election campaign, pointing out, for example, that statistically insignificant differences in reported voting intentions between polls taken at different times were being misrepresented as indicating important shifts in the electorate's mood. Those blogs themselves may have been of interest to a relatively restricted portion of the general public. However, they were certainly taken notice of by the members of the press on which they were commenting, who engaged with their critics in a spirited dialogue about the merits of their behavior. The existence of such dialogue is itself a welcome development, indicating that not only are the mainstream media likely to become more ethically self-conscious as a result of the monitoring and reporting of the blogs, but that the blogs themselves are also likely to be held to high standards by the mainstream media.

Regulation of Ownership

A good deal of the discussion of the regulation of the media has focused not on the question of content, such as how the media comes to gain information and the ways in which they use the information which they do have, but on issues surrounding the structure of ownership within the industry. For much of the twentieth century, there was a seemingly inexorable trend towards fewer and fewer media outlets being controlled by fewer and larger companies. At one time each town of any size supported at least one newspaper, typically locally owned, and cities had a number of daily newspapers, but over time most of the newspapers went out of existence, and the ownership of those that remained tended to fall into the hands of large conglomerates.[4]

Of course, in any industry there are legitimate concerns about unhealthy concentration of ownership, since effective competition is a condition for a properly functioning market. In the case of the debate about concentration of ownership in the media industry, however, the concerns go beyond this. These concerns belong in two broad classes. First, there are fears that the ownership structure of the media industry will impact adversely on the content of the media. Second, there are fears that it will give media proprietors undue political influence.

Let us begin by outlining the specific fears concerning content. In the first place, it is thought that large media conglomerates are likely to allow commercial norms to dominate media norms inappropriately (see discussion in Chapter 3) by, for example, refusing to present minority or unpopular views if these are likely to alienate consumers. It is also thought that content will become undesirably homogenized. One worry is that in a media dominated by a few large players it will become more difficult for different views and groups to be heard, that is, there will be a decrease in diversity. Another worry is that such a media is less likely to play a public service role. For a key function of the media is transmitting messages of immediate public interest, such as warnings of extreme weather or of natural or human disasters, providing space for political debates, or, on a more homely level, making announcements about "what's on," allowing charities, civic associations, and so on to promote their activities.

Now let us consider the fear that, with greater concentration of media ownership, will come undue political influence. It is thought that such influence will be used either to promote the owners' own political views, or to pressurize politicians to formulate media policies which favor the interests of current media owners, or both.

A common response to fears of both these kinds is to advocate that the government act to overcome them, either by bringing in regulation which aims to restrict media concentration, or by setting up state-supported media organizations, or both. Before looking at these responses, however, we should consider the validity of the fears that prompt them. Again, we begin with those which concern the impact on media content. The first of these is that large media conglomerates are likely to allow commercial norms to inappropriately dominate media norms. As we pointed out in Chapter 3, there is in principle no reason why a media organization cannot act in accordance with media norms and at the same time be a thriving business enterprise. Counter-intuitively, there are reasons for supposing that it is actually easier for media norms to be respected when ownership is concentrated than when it is not. Consider a situation where three rival television stations compete in a local area. Each will try to appeal to as many people as possible. This is likely to have two related effects: each of the stations will be quite similar to the others, and each will seek to occupy the middle ground, not broadcasting anything that might offend or disturb many of its viewers. Now imagine the same area when a single company has come to own all three stations. It makes no sense for that company to compete against itself by having similar programming on all three channels. Rather, it can dedicate one station to satisfying mainstream tastes, while broadcasting material on the other two that appeals to more specialized minority audiences, without fear of thereby alienating the bulk of its audience. Hence, at least in some cases, a decrease in diversity of ownership might actually produce an increase in diversity of content. Moreover, it may be that the taste or opinions of the majority may be affected by their exposure to alternative material.

If this line of thought is persuasive, it shows that more concentrated media ownership does not inevitably have a negative impact on diversity. There is in fact now a good deal of evidence to show that there is no straightforward correlation between the growth in conglomerate ownership of media outlets and less (or more) diversity in viewpoints or, for that matter, in quality of material presented or local content.[5] Arguably, there is an ongoing problem with lack of representation of diversity in the media, which stems not simply from the ownership structure of particular outlets, but also from the fact that almost all such outlets face the same commercial pressures. However, as we saw in Chapter 6, even if concentration of ownership does not necessarily have a negative impact on diversity of viewpoints and quality of material, the power imbalance which comes with such concentration can be, and, on occasions, has been, misused.

Concerns about the undue political influence that comes with great media power do seem to be well founded. We know that media interests lobby aggressively to promote their commercial interests. Of course, this in itself makes media organizations no different from other commercial groups. What does distinguish them from most other such groups is the power they possess to punish politicians who do not act as they wish. That power, moreover, becomes greater every time they are given preferential treatment. The thought that a healthy democracy depends on an independent relationship between the media and political spheres cuts both ways: just as politicians should not be able to use the media to entrench their political power, the media should not be able to use political influence to entrench their economic power, or to make their own political views carry extra weight. Identifying the problem is one thing, but coming up with an effective and morally and politically feasible solution is another.

State-supported media organizations, such as the BBC in the United Kingdom and the ABC in Australia, provide a possible offset to the unbridled political power of large media groups. These organizations are funded by the state, but are statutory bodies which are not controlled by the government of the day. As such they avoid (in theory, at least) the problems which beset the relationship between commercial media organizations and governments. They can stand above the fray, reporting and commenting on the activities of both the government and commercial media. Furthermore, since they are not driven by the same financial imperatives as the commercial media, they are more able to present minority views.[6]

Historically, an important tool that governments have possessed to regulate media ownership is their control over access to the electromagnetic spectrum. Much of that spectrum – used to carry radio broadcasts, television transmissions, and the like – is characterized by two features which make such restriction of access necessary. First, it is non-excludable, in that anyone with the right kind of technology can use it. Second, it is congestible, that is, if more than a certain number (often one) of users try to use the same part of the spectrum they will interfere with each other. The spectrum is a natural phenomenon, arguably to be seen as a public asset, which should be used so as to be of greatest benefit to society as a whole. So it seems reasonable that it be the government that decides the terms of access to the spectrum.

The enormous importance of the broadcast media in the twentieth and twenty-first centuries has meant that governments, as gatekeepers to the electromagnetic spectrum, have been able to exert a considerable degree of control over both the content and the ownership of the media. This is true even in the USA, where the First Amendment's requirement that "Congress shall make no law" to abridge "freedom of speech, or of the press" has effectively kept the government from direct regulation of newspapers. Since 1934, in order to operate, US broadcasters have required government-issued licenses, which must be renewed every few years. To gain such licenses broadcasters are supposed to demonstrate conformity to "public interest" requirements, including programming children's shows and responding to local concerns, as well restricting their use of "risqué language." Importantly, broadcasters have not been allowed to own a large number of stations[7] or newspapers in the same cities where they have TV stations, so the political influence of their owners can be kept within bounds. Other countries such as Canada and Australia have had similar systems in place, with restrictions on cross-media ownership.

Wherever they exist, such restrictions have come under considerable and increasing pressure over the past few decades. Some of this pressure reflects the growing influence of neo-liberal thought, with its suspicion of government regulation generally. Some is specific to the media. In particular, the growth of a wide variety of channels of transmission of information (including some which do not rely on access to the electromagnetic spectrum such as cable TV), many of them with relatively low "entry costs," is making it possible for a far wider range of groups than in the past to gain access to media platforms for the spreading of their message. That is, it is held both that there is less need for the government to exert control over the media than there was in the past, since technological developments are bringing about the results that government was aiming at, in particular diversity of viewpoint; and there is less possibility of such control being successful, since it is no longer possible to control access to channels of communication in the way it was in the past. Whether, and the extent to which, both of these claims are true remains to be seen.

Conclusion

As we pointed out in earlier chapters, there are moral demands built into the functions which define the media, that is, gathering and disseminating information. While there is no reason to believe that media workers and organizations are any less morally well motivated than others – indeed, many have behaved in morally admirable ways – the media faces particular problems in its attempts to build regulatory structures to try to ensure that those demands are met. First, the commercial pressures that bear down on most media organizations generate incentives to ignore and override moral considerations. But, second, the fundamental importance of a free press means that it is undesirable that the government intervene to set and enforce standards as it does in other industries where such pressures are likely to subvert good intentions. At the same time, freedom of the press means that in the face of the growth of diverse channels of communication and of "citizen journalists," who operate beyond the control of established media organizations, it is becoming even more difficult for those organizations themselves to control the behavior of practitioners, even when they sincerely want to. These are the real challenges facing those who would promote moral behavior in media workers.

195

However, we have reason to think that these attempts can be effective, if properly conceived and executed. For example, the increasing diversity and accessibility of channels of media communication is making it easier for the behavior of media organizations and individual media workers to be monitored, and to be held to account if it falls short. In the case of individual members of the media, such accountability draws on and reinforces existing professional ethical attitudes; in the case of media organizations, it makes use of their desire to retain a commercial reputation as a reliable purveyor of information.

Chapter study questions

1. Why is self-regulation especially desirable in the case of the media? Even if it is desirable, why is it problematic?
2. One of the concerns often raised about the increasing control of the media by large conglomerates is that they are likely to allow commercial norms to inappropriately dominate media norms. Give two examples of such inappropriate domination. Is there good reason to worry that this will actually happen?
3. Give two examples of arrangements which are likely to promote ethical behavior in the media.
4. Are there reasons to think that the growth of the new media is likely to undermine media ethics? Are there reasons to think that it is likely to promote media ethics?
5. In your view, are there good reasons to have restrictions on cross-media ownership (e.g., forbidding someone owning both a TV station and a newspaper in the same city)?

Notes

1. This code of ethics can be found at http://www.alliance.org.au/code-of-ethics.html.
2. See, e.g., the discussion in Harding 2010.
3. Examples were www.mumble.com.au/ and www.crikey.com.au/ commentariat/Possum-Comitatus.html.

4. There is dispute as to whether the media industry is actually more concentrated than it was in the past, particularly in the light of the growth of alternative media channels over the last decade. See Napoli (2006). What cannot be denied is the growth of very large media conglomerates, such as AOL-Warner.
5. This evidence is well summarized in Gamson and Latteier (2004).
6. In Australia, for example, the government supports the Special Broadcasting Service, whose mission is to "provide multilingual and multicultural radio and television services that inform, educate and entertain all Australians and, in doing so, reflect Australia's multicultural society."
7. In one sense, there is diffused ownership of television stations in the USA, with some 700 local television news stations, for example, owned by over 100 different companies. But since more than 90 percent of these stations are affiliates of one of the "Big Four" TV networks (ABC, CBS, Fox, and NBC), this diffusion does not necessarily translate into diversity of viewpoint (Project for Excellence in Journalism 2007).

References

Australian Press Council (2008) Statement of principles. http://www.presscouncil.org.au/pcsite/complaints/sop.html, accessed Nov. 10, 2010.

Bertrand, Claude-Jean (2000) *Media Ethics and Accountability Systems.* New Brunswick, NJ: Transaction Publishers.

Bowen, Shannon (2004) Organisational factors encouraging ethical decision making: an exploration into the case of an exemplar. *Journal of Business Ethics*, 52(4), 311–324.

Gamson, J., and Latteier, P. (2004) Do media monsters devour diversity? *Contexts*, 3(3), 26–32.

Harding, Evan (2010) The funding journalism conundrum. Upstart, Sept. 6. http://www.upstart.net.au/2010/09/06/the-funding-journalism-conundru/, accessed Nov. 16, 2010.

Kiplinger, Knight (2005) Who's watching the watchdog? *Ethics Resource Center.* http://www.ethics.org/resource/whos-watching-watchdog, accessed Nov. 10, 2010.

Napoli, Philip M. (ed.) (2006) *Media Diversity and Localism: Meaning And Metrics* New York: Routledge.

Newton, L., Hodges, L., and Keith, S. (2004) Accountability in the professions. *Journal of Mass Media Ethics*, 19(3–4), 166–190.

Project for Excellence in Journalism (2007) *The State of the News Media 2007*. http://www.stateofthenewsmedia.org/2007/narrative_localtv_ownership.asp?cat=4&media=7, accessed Nov. 10, 2010.

USA Communication Act (1934) http://www.medialaw.ru/laws/other_ laws/american/ca1934-e.htm, accessed Nov. 10, 2010.

9

Moral Excellence and Role Models in the Media

Introduction

In this chapter, we examine role models in the media, with regard to their effectiveness in acting as ethical motivators. If we learn from those we love (or at least, those whom we respect) role models may provide additional motivation for ethical conduct, which will minimize proportionally the requirement for external compliance through regulation. In a free market economy where media organizations are run as businesses, ethical role models could potentially enhance the moral standing and effectiveness of self-regulation and render external compliance through regulation, the bane of a free economy, less necessary.

The chapter begins from the premise that the media plays an important role in carrying a society's stories to the people of that society. The storytelling or bardic function of the media is an essential part of cultural life. Writing for the UK newspaper the

Media, Markets, and Morals, First Edition. Edward H. Spence, Andrew Alexandra, Aaron Quinn, and Anne Dunn.
© 2011 Edward H. Spence, Andrew Alexandra, Aaron Quinn, and Anne Dunn.
Published 2011 by Blackwell Publishing Ltd.

Daily Telegraph, the British chief rabbi Jonathan Sacks suggests that "[a] culture is defined by its narratives" and storytelling is "the vehicle of continuity" in bringing people together as a community (Sacks 2001).

If we accept this, then obviously the storyteller matters as much as the stories themselves. Whether a story celebrates diversity or cultivates mistrust, for example, reflects the choices of the storyteller; in journalistic terms, this means the angle the writer chooses. The difference between the choices has an ethical dimension. David Randall argues that "there are only two kinds of journalism: good and bad ... [Good] journalism ... is, in every sense of the word, universal," calling his book *The Universal Journalist* (Randall 2000, viii). Randall's view of journalism is thus one that echoes the universal principles elaborated in Chapter 2 under *universal public morality*, such as Kant's categorical imperative and Gewirth's principle of generic consistency.

Of course, not only journalists but also other media practitioners such as advertisers, or those whose work is in public relations, may tell their society's stories in ways that are morally admirable, or morally dubious. We expect our media to tell the truth (to be as accurate as possible in the telling of a story and not to mislead or misinform) and to treat both sources and audience with respect and honesty (not as means to an end). Another way of putting this is that media practitioners should aim to act in ways that are morally excellent.

Accordingly, this chapter asks a number of questions, such as: What is meant by moral excellence? How can morally excellent media practice be encouraged? Is unethical behavior in the professions "a matter of human frailty," or one of systemic failure (Dickinson 2007, 200, citing Becker 1970)? The central argument of the chapter is that *role models* are important in the education of media practitioners. The final section of the chapter offers four examples: legendary US journalist Edward R. Murrow, respected Australian journalist Chris Masters, and two women, Veronica Guerin and Anna Politkovskaya, who paid with their lives for informing the public under dangerous circumstances. All, in different ways, displayed courage, which was identified earlier in this book as one of the *cardinal virtues*. In the case of one of them, however, there is a question as to whether her courage could better be described as foolhardiness, and thus as setting a wrong example to others.

Moral Excellence

Chapter 4 made a connection between professionalism and ethics. Professionalism in this sense means a high level of competence in the performance of professional functions. The connection is in the proposal that highly competent media practice is essential to ethical practice, that in effect they are one and the same. Karen Sanders has explored this connection in detail, asserting that "ethically good journalism begins with competent reporting" (2003, 160). Her approach is part of a twenty-first-century resurgence of interest in *virtue ethics*, which have their origin in the work of the Greek philosophers, in particular the writings of Aristotle (384–322 BCE), and their interpretation by the thirteenth-century Christian scholar, St. Thomas Aquinas.

Virtue theory was described in some detail in Chapter 4, in relation to professionalism. This chapter revisits the theory in order to consider how morally excellent media practitioners might emerge. The emphasis in virtue ethics is on character rather than on principles from which moral judgments can be deduced. People must therefore be practiced in virtuous action in order to be able to judge right and wrong. By behaving virtuously, we acquire the virtues. Each virtue lies at "the golden mean" between two vices: one of excess and one of deficiency. Thus, courage is the ideal between cowardice and foolhardiness, magnanimity between meanness and profligacy. Aristotle claimed that, in order to know how to judge where virtue lies and to have the correct foundation to live a moral life, people must have a good education (including their upbringing). You must live right to know what is right, rather than learning what is right in principle so as to live by those principles. Thus, the strength of virtue ethics is its substantive account of an ideal *role morality*. This term refers to Aristotle's belief that every art and activity has an aim or goal, for a particular good: "the end of the medical art is health, that of shipbuilding a vessel, that of strategy victory, that of economics wealth" (Aristotle 350 BCE, bk I, ch. 1).

What is the aim of journalism? For Belsey and Chadwick (1992, 1) it is "the circulation of information, including news, comment and opinion," upon which the health of a community – especially one with "any pretensions to democracy" – depends. For Sanders (2003, 161) it includes not only the providing of information but also "the scrutiny of the powerful" and "revelation of injustice," as well as "providing a voice for all sectors of society." Yet another definition has the aim of journalism as "contributing to public discourse by providing factual, reliable, timely and meaningful information" (Hayes et al. 2007, 265). In other words, it is an activity in the service of the public, to enable discussion and participation in public affairs. The important thing to note is that "for journalism to be good, it must have good aims" (Sanders 2003, 161). The same could be said of other media professions, such as advertising and public relations. For Aristotle, the good person is a happy and fulfilled one. Since it is the aim of human beings to be happy, this makes behaving virtuously a rational choice. As we shall see, behaving as a virtuous journalist may bring mixed blessings, and can have tragic consequences for individual journalists.

Moral excellence is thus both a function of individual character and of the profession itself in terms of its aims. Character is formed through education and through actions that over time form habits of behavior or, in the professional context, professional routines and practices. In this view, the effectiveness of professional codes of ethics lies mostly in "creating climates of opinion and control mechanisms to ensure that flawed characters become *professionally unacceptable*" (Sanders 2003, 162; emphasis original). Another way of putting this is that you simply cannot be a good journalist (or any other media practitioner) unless you practice the virtues of your profession. Professional routines and practices constitute both a social and an ethical framework; indeed, all ethical decisions have to be made within contextual frameworks. Context requires judgment as to the right behavior. Sanders (2003, 16) uses the example of courage: for a journalist to go into a war zone or to pursue an investigation into the activities of violent criminals may be courageous under one set of circumstances (the significance of the story, the preparations made) but foolhardy under others.

Context can make conflicting demands on individuals that make it very hard to reach a decision about how best to act. A majority of media professionals are employed in organizations that are also businesses, which rely on earning sufficient to fund their continued existence. This may lead to individual practitioners coming under pressure from their employers to cut ethical corners in the pursuit of profit. In such situations, a strong hold on the virtues of professional practice is essential, and this is learned through right upbringing and education, and through experience. One aspect of experience is maturation; psychologists have proposed that moral judgment develops in stages, as – and only so far as – the individual matures. Major news organizations may enjoy a reputation for credible, trustworthy information, and this is likely both to benefit journalists who work for that organization and to identify individual employees who undermine that reputation through unethical behavior as aberrant. From an ethical point of view, however, an individual must exercise personal moral responsibility to attain moral excellence, and cannot derive it from an organization (Hayes et al. 2007, 270).

Twentieth-century psychologists, as much as philosophers, have considered exactly how it is that an individual ethical framework or personal moral code develops. Some, such as Lawrence Kohlberg (1981), believe that moral development occurs in stages that everyone must go through, in the same order; that is, there is a hierarchy of development from most immature to fully mature. Kohlberg was influenced by the work of Swiss cognitive psychologist Jean Piaget (1968), who proposed four stages of development, from concrete thinking in infancy to abstract thinking, which develops from about the ages of 11 or 12. These shifts over time also demonstrate a movement from egocentric thinking (the infant and young child are unable to imagine things from another's point of view) to more "decentered" thinking, incorporating being able to put oneself "in someone else's shoes." Kohlberg applied Piaget's theory to moral development at three levels: the pre-conventional, which lasts until about age 9, the conventional, which characterizes the rest of childhood into early adulthood, and post-conventional, which may never be attained at all. In the first stage, the child attempts only to avoid punishment and to gain rewards. In the second, long (and perhaps permanent) stage, the individual learns to recognize and abide by (or to flout) rules and laws of all kinds, from games to legal constraints. Moral decisions are based on issues of duty and rules, in this stage. Only at the final, post-conventional, level do people act on the basis of personal moral standards and according to social contracts or mutually agreed codes incorporating rights and obligations. Kohlberg's is thus an ethics of *justice*.

One of Kohlberg's students, Carol Gilligan (1982), noticed that on some of Kohlberg's tests, women scored lower than men. He was not the first psychologist to argue that women's morality is deficient compared to men's: both Freud and Erik Erikson had also reached this conclusion, believing that women were incapable of developing the same levels of moral maturity as men, so long as they remained emotionally attached to mother and family. Inability to separate from the mother was a sign of arrested development, in this view. Gilligan conducted her own investigations and produced another stage theory, different from Kohlberg's. Gilligan's theory argues that women have not an inferior, but a different, process of moral development. It is one that focuses on relationships and connection, not separation, on an ethic not of justice, but of care. Development over time is in one's sense of self in relation to others, passing from selfishness to responsibility and thence (and, again, this final stage may not reached by some) to a stance of equal respect and concern for self and others. Subsequent research has shown this approach to moral decision-making is not unique to women; men and women may use both justice and care as principles in their moral reasoning. Gilligan has also been criticized for overlooking differences between Western and other cultures in socialization and therefore values. But her work was groundbreaking not only in that it demonstrated the inadequacy of a male-centered view (Kohlberg based his theory on interviews only with men) but also in its reconnection of ethical decision-making with both the individual sense of self and the social context.

The "ethics of care" has a parallel in the "disinterested service" that is included in one definition of professionalism. In relation to media professionals and the development of moral excellence, there can be little doubt of the centrality of learning what constitutes ethically good practice, which raises the question of how best to educate journalists and other media practitioners. This is the question we turn to now.

Educating Media Practitioners: A Place for Role Models

The education of media practitioners today takes place much more often in universities than it did 20 or 30 years ago. Journalism in particular was characterized by a system of socialization into the role through on-the-job training. Even today, about half of new recruits to journalism or public relations will not have completed a communication or journalism degree, although they are likely to have a university degree in another field. At a time when journalism schools in the USA were well established, popular with students, and, in many cases, respected by the profession, James Carey made a forceful argument against the "professional" degree and in favor of educating journalists in the humanities and social sciences (Carey 1980). In 2003, Lee Bollinger, the President of Columbia University, home of the Pulitzer Prize for journalism, issued a statement at the end of a series of meetings of a task force he had convened "to consider the question of what a model school of journalism for the Twenty-first Century should look like" (Bollinger 2003). In his statement, Bollinger embraced journalism as a profession, and universities as playing an important role in the preparation of individuals to enter the profession. However, universities should "always stand at a certain distance from the profession itself" and be "the profession's loyal critics." In enumerating the "basic capacities" that a journalism school should instill in its students, Bollinger included both familiarity with the history of their field and its great figures, and "the moral and ethical standards that should guide professional behavior" (Bollinger 2003). In so saying, the Columbia University president was acknowledging the importance both of education in ethical behavior and of role models.

We learn what is considered right and wrong in interaction with others (parents, friends, teachers, colleagues). All of them are in some respects role models, not all necessarily good ones. There are, after all, unethical practitioners – quacks and crooks – in every profession. When it comes to selecting good role models, some people may be inclined to think that media professions such as journalism, public relations, or advertising would find this hard to do. Moreover, it may not be easy to find a single role model who is wholly and unequivocally virtuous because human beings are very complicated. It can be instructive, however, to give consideration to whether or not a particular practitioner might be called a good role model for the profession. Let us consider some examples from journalism.

Edward R. Murrow (1908–1965)

This legendary American journalist was a pioneer of television news broadcasting, having established his reputation for truthful and courageous reporting in a series of radio broadcasts for CBS during World War II. Murrow was also a powerful mentor not only to journalists but also to the camera operators and producers who worked with him. He recruited a team of journalists who became known in the industry as "Murrow's Boys" (few women were working as broadcast correspondents in the 1930s and 1940s). During his regular broadcasts for CBS from London during the Blitz, Morrow developed a signature sign-off that later became the title of a 2005 movie (2005; dir. G. Clooney): "Good night, and good luck." Early in the 1950s Murrow and his producer Fred Friendly took to television a current affairs format they had introduced on radio as *Hear It Now*, calling it, reasonably enough, *See It Now*. This was very early in the life of television as a mass medium, and Murrow introduced his new series with the words "This is an old team, trying to learn a new trade." Murrow was already a role model for broadcast journalists, celebrated for his honesty and integrity, virtues of character that he was to demonstrate in his new medium.

It was a time to challenge the ethics of any citizen, never mind any journalist. The United States and its allies were in the grip of the Cold War, with the Soviet Union and all forms of communism perceived as a direct threat to democracy and to the principle of freedom. At the height of the Cold War, in 1953 and 1954, Senator Joseph McCarthy used his position as chairman of the Senate Permanent Subcommittee on Investigations to launch an anti-communist crusade, subpoenaing witnesses on short notice and often being the only senator to attend closed-door hearings. If witnesses invoked the Fifth Amendment of the US Constitution, which protects against self-incrimination, McCarthy would call them "Fifth Amendment communists" and if he thought he could intimidate them, would make witnesses appear in public to be cross-examined by him. Transcripts of hearings, released in 2003, showed that McCarthy manipulated hearings by calling only witnesses he could intimidate and avoiding those likely to stand up to him. The coining of the term "McCarthyism" to describe this kind of persecutionary anti-communist fervor, which characterized the whole era, demonstrates the pervasiveness of the senator's influence on American society. A journalist working with Murrow at the time has described it thus: "You had to live through the times to know how fearful – indeed, terrorized – people were about speaking their minds. The cold war with Russia, the threat of a hot war with China, security programs and loyalty oaths – all had cowed the citizens of the most powerful nation on earth into keeping their minds closed and their mouths shut. The Senate of the United States, in order not to appear Red, chose to be yellow. It was the Age of McCarthyism. Edward R. Murrow helped bring it to an end" (Wershba n.d.).

The special edition of *See It Now* that Murrow broadcast on March 9, 1954, called "A report on Senator Joseph McCarthy," is credited with beginning a backlash against McCarthy that would end his reign of terror. It was a courageous act, because Murrow had been warned only a few months earlier that McCarthy had evidence of his having been "on the Soviet payroll." This turned out to refer to an incident in the early 1930s, when the young Murrow had worked for an organization called the Institute of International Education (IIE) in New York. In 1934, the IIE had organized an exchange between American academics and their Soviet counterparts. This was enough for McCarthy to have subpoenaed Murrow. There was an added, implicit threat to the career of Murrow's brother, who was a general in the US Air Force (see Wershba n.d.). Given the level of fear Wershba describes above, Murrow showed both courage and practical judgment (in virtue theory, *phronesis*) in the way he and his team carefully researched and delivered their report, specifically targeting McCarthy. He is often quoted as having had doubts about using the power of television to attack an individual but reached an ethical decision that we can call consequentialist, that is, revealing McCarthy's manipulative behaviour, exaggerations, and inconsistencies led to the greater public good. The network, CBS, would not permit Murrow and Friendly, his producer, to use CBS money to advertise the program, or to use the network logo in the ads, so the journalist and his producer paid for newspaper advertisements themselves. After the broadcast, tens of thousands of letters, telegrams, and phone calls poured into CBS, running 15 to 1 in Murrow's favor. In December of that year, the US Senate voted to censure Joseph McCarthy, making him one of the few senators ever to be so disciplined; he died in hospital three years later.

Edward R. Murrow is still considered one of journalism's greatest role models. In the movie *The Insider* (1999; dir. M. Mann), a television producer who succumbs to advertiser pressure to tone down a piece of investigative journalism exposing unethical behavior in the tobacco industry, is accused of "betraying the legacy of Edward R. Murrow." What makes Murrow an excellent role model is that his actions exemplify the cardinal virtues and are evidence of his practical wisdom. In Murrow we see that combination of justification, motivation, and internal compliance, described in Chapter 2 as giving rise to personal, individual ethical conduct.

Chris Masters

This Australian television reporter has already been mentioned in Chapter 4, in relation to a program broadcast in 1987 called "The moonlight state" which rocked the country. It instigated a Royal Commission (known as the Fitzgerald Inquiry) into police corruption in the Australian state of Queensland, which in turn produced a large number of convictions of corruption in the police, including of a former Queensland police commissioner, Sir Terence Lewis. Masters has written that what he discovered about the extent and nature of police corruption severely tested his fundamental belief "that people are basically good" (1992, 47).

In the account of his investigation that Masters wrote some years later, he talks about the danger that police beat reporters were becoming reluctant to probe too deeply the sources on which they relied for their daily stories, and of the way in which, over time, they became too close to "the people they have to deal with every day, the police themselves" (1992, 55). This is a form of corruption (see Chapter 6), which Masters recognized and was able to resist, despite his dependence on his sources for information. He became aware that the police in Brisbane (Queensland's capital city and the place Masters was conducting his research) were watching him closely and quite possibly monitoring his telephone calls. He recounts how, time and again, people who knew the state's police force was corrupt, told him there was nothing he could do about it. Masters would not give in to defeatism, because he held it to be his "professional responsibility" to expose as much of the wrongdoing as possible. This exemplifies the role morality discussed in Chapter 4.

Although the final television program, aired as part of the investigative documentary series *Four Corners*, by the national public service broadcaster, the Australian Broadcasting Corporation, can certainly be held to have improved the moral integrity of the nation through exposing a corrupt police culture, Masters and the ABC were to face more than a decade of legal action as a result of Australia's defamation laws. As a result, despite still believing that what he did was worthwhile, Masters has expressed concern that the price of "the death by a thousand courts" was too high to encourage young journalists to follow his example (Masters 2001).

There are examples aplenty of Masters' courage. He recounts how close he came to being set up on a trumped-up charge that would nevertheless have ruined his reputation. There is also an illustration of how his own courage inspired courage in others, namely the seven key witnesses who eventually agreed to be filmed for the program, all of whom put themselves at risk by doing so. Masters acknowledges that the risks of the investigation "were not just mine to take" and recounts a moment when he inadvertently put another witness in danger. He argues that "there are times when you can't help but take chances in order to get a little closer to the truth." Veronica Guerin, whose case is recounted below, would certainly have endorsed this argument. But perhaps a key difference between Masters and Guerin can be found in what Masters goes on to write: "Any person who takes their work seriously is most likely prepared to take sensible, professional `risks'" (Masters 1992:68). Here we have the challenge of right judgment, of knowing the difference between risk that is "sensible, professional" and risk that is not.

Veronica Guerin

The case of this Irish journalist, murdered by drug dealers in 1996, illustrates the complexity of role models. Her name became internationally known after Australian actress Cate Blanchett played the title role in the 2003 movie, *Veronica Guerin* (dir. J. Schumacher). Guerin had been a renowned and fearless crime reporter for the Irish *Sunday Independent* newspaper. Over the two years prior to her death she had been investigating drugs gangs in Dublin. Two drug dealers were found guilty of her murder. Her reports had seriously hampered the illegal operations of the drugs gangs, and the judge who sentenced her killers said her death had not been in vain, because of the many young people her work had spared "the scourge of drugs" (Laville 1999). Guerin would confront those whom she was investigating, going to their homes alone to interview them; on one occasion, in 1995, she was attacked and beaten by a man said to be the boss of the Dublin drugs gang that murdered her a year later. In 1994 a shot was fired into her home through a window; she was shot at her front door the following year but survived; and after she was beaten, the same man called her and threatened to kidnap and rape her young son. Her newspaper installed a security system to protect her and the Garda (Irish police) gave her a 24-hour escort, which Guerin said hampered her work.

In the 2003 film about her, Guerin is clearly meant to be seen as heroic; indeed, the director of the film alluded to her as a real-life hero. At the time of Guerin's death, her editor described her in heroic terms: "She insisted on the freedom to do her job and, armed only with her pen, she set about doing that" (Muir 1996). But Guerin was also a wife and mother; her son was six years old when she died. Some argued that for her to continue her investigative work after such violence and threat was not courageous but "reckless" (Taylor 2003). In a book published two years after her death, the author Emily O'Reilly accused Guerin of putting her son at risk and of "blurr[ing] the line between journalist and detective" (BBC News 1998). After the 1994 shooting, Guerin and her husband reportedly discussed whether or not she should continue such dangerous work, Guerin concluding: "But I thought, what was the point of giving in to them? That's what they want. Then they'll think that they can just continue doing it to everybody else. So I carried on" (Muir 1996). When she was shot in 1995, she said, "I vow that the eyes of justice, the eyes of this journalist will not be shut again. No hand can deter me from my battle for the truth" (IPI n.d.).

Here we appear to have an example of a journalist determined to inform the public, to reveal the truth about what was happening in society. Her death was met with widespread shock and a response that identified it with the moral role of journalism. The Irish prime minister called it "an attack on democracy" and a joint statement of prominent newspaper editors in Ireland and England spoke of her murder as "a fundamental attack on the free press." Their statement concluded: "Journalists will not be intimidated." And Guerin did make a difference. After her death, the Irish government launched its biggest ever criminal investigation, eventually changing the law to give it the power to seize assets bought with the proceeds of crime and to prevent criminals from benefiting financially from their crimes. In Veronica Guerin, we have a case study of the complexity of acting virtuously in the Aristotelian sense described at the beginning of the chapter, and of the importance of contextual factors.

Anna Politkovskaya

This Russian journalist was an outspoken critic of the war in Chechnya. She was found shot dead in her apartment building in Moscow in October 2006. Chechnya is a Muslim republic trying to break away from Moscow; Russia has waged two wars against it since the mid-1990s. Politkovskaya's reporting on Chechnya began in 1999, at the start of the second of these wars. She concentrated her attention on the impact of the fighting on the civilian population, on the brutal behavior of both the Russian and the Chechen forces. She was one of the few people to enter the Moscow theater where Chechen militants took hundreds hostage, in 2002. Politkovskaya documented the killing, torture, and beating of civilians. She was not afraid to name those she accused, such as Russian police officer Sergei Lapin. He was detained, but the case was dismissed, and Politkovskaya had made another enemy. Foreign journalists based in Moscow, and other Russian journalists were united in the view that Politkovskaya was "in a class of her own" and "the first name that came to mind" as an example of honest journalism in Russia (Observer 2006).

Despite repeated threats to her life, Politkovskaya would not be silenced, nor did she think of herself as a hero, saying, "I'm just trying to do my job, to let people know what's happening in our country" (Parfitt 2006). Thus, like Guerin, she drew attention to the aim or goal of journalism as her own moral compass. Her stand was the more remarkable because so few journalists in Russia, working largely for state-owned or controlled publications, were prepared to report on events in Chechnya. International news agencies were grateful for the information only she was brave enough to make public. Politkovskaya received international awards for her writing, but also criticism that her journalism was biased against Russia and President Vladimir Putin. Her defenders countered that she was as willing to expose Chechen rebel tactics as to criticize the Russian forces. After her death, Politkovskaya was mourned by thousands of ordinary Russians, who held vigils in Moscow and St. Petersburg. There seemed little doubt in the minds of the people there as to who had killed her. Written across a giant photograph of her in Pushkin Square, Moscow were the words "The Kremlin has killed freedom of speech" and on another photo, of President Putin, "You are responsible for everything" (Blomfield 2006).

In June 2008, news agencies reported that three men had been charged in Moscow with involvement in Politkovskaya's murder, but the assassin remained at large (Sydney Morning Herald 2008). The three men (two Chechen brothers and a former Moscow police officer) were acquitted by jury, but in June 2009 the Supreme Court overturned this verdict and ordered a retrial. News agencies reported that the original trial "was widely seen as an embarrassing farce" (*Sydney Morning Herald*, June 27–28, 2009), with key evidence left out or going missing. At the time of writing, Politkovskaya's family were calling for a total reinvestigation of her murder.

Conclusion

This chapter has put forward the idea that "moral excellence" in professional behavior is closely connected to excellent professional practice. It can be a source of moral excellence to do an important job – such as journalism – well. If it is to reside anywhere, moral excellence must do so in individuals, who take ultimate responsibility for ethical decision-making, no matter how ethically excellent (or corrupt) an organization might be. Individuals develop moral frameworks over time and through socialization, including education. The kind of education appropriate to professionals is not universally agreed upon, but if it is to contribute to the moral education of individuals, it must surely go beyond technical training. It needs to encompass knowledge and appreciation of the history of the profession and its conceptual frameworks, and of those whose contribution is widely acknowledged as epitomizing its goals and principles. This is where role models can provide a valuable starting point for reflection. The cases of Veronica Guerin and Anna Politkovskaya demonstrate that even the apparently heroic pursuit of truth and its disclosure in the face of threats and intimidation may not always be simply as virtuous as they seem.

In the foreword to Masters' book, his former executive producer, Jonathan Holmes, writes of the reporter's honesty, and of his "anger." It is a righteous anger, driven by a desire to see justice done. Murrow shared the same anger, as did Guerin and Politkovskaya. In Chapter 4, we argued that justice ought to be a governing virtue for journalists. The journalists discussed here all display that virtue, and as such, offer positive role models to all media professionals.

The concept of the role model offered in this concluding chapter of the book connects directly with arguments made in the first part of the book. These began by establishing what ethical reasoning is. Three elements make up ethical reasoning: justification, motivation, and compliance. The individual or the organization that has internalized these three will be capable of ethical decision-making, through acknowledging the rationale for ethical behavior and being motivated by those arguments to comply with these justified ethical principles, through either internal or external compliance. The justified ethical principles put forward in Chapter 2 together make up a universal public morality, within which all of us must operate if we are to live ethically. Acknowledging the superior power of this global, public ethical framework, media professionals have a primary role to disseminate information – which itself has an inherent normative structure – and this role determines their professional ethical framework, or role morality. The good role model, then, demonstrates both the virtues that characterize the role morality of his or her profession and an understanding, demonstrated in actions and beliefs, of what is universally right and good. In the media professions, this role morality lies in a character that automatically and consistently demonstrates, in the exercise of his or her profession, honesty and accuracy, sincerity, fairness, and courage. These in turn exemplify the universal ethical principles of truthfulness and justice. It would be unrealistic to expect all media professionals to display all of these virtues all of the time, but those who consistently act according to even one of the key principles are likely to provide a better role model than those who cannot or will not do so.

Chapter study questions

1. Discuss the proposition that the moral excellence of the story-teller is as important as the ethics of the story.
2. "There are only two kinds of journalism ... good and bad" (David Randall, *The Universal Journalist*). What did Randall mean when he wrote this?
3. What might be a special challenge for journalists in behaving virtuously? What is its equivalent for other media practitioners, such as public relations or advertising professionals?
4. This chapter states that it is not enough for organizations to act ethically to guarantee ethical behavior in their employees. Do you agree? How important is it that organizations are ethical in their practices?
5. Discuss the differences between an ethics of justice and an ethics of care. Do you agree that there may be a relationship between gender and ethical development?
6. How does the example of McCarthyism illustrate the importance of good role models? Can you think of other historical or contemporary examples in which a courageous role model might have made a difference?
7. This chapter suggests that Guerin took risks that did not demonstrate right judgment, unlike Murrow, Masters, and even Politkovskaya. Do you agree? What differences are there between the behavior of these four, in terms of their approach to risk for themselves and for others?

References

Aristotle (350 BCE) *Nicomachean Ethics*, ed. and trans. W. D. Ross. http://classics.mit.edu/Aristotle/nicomachaen.html, accessed Nov. 12, 2010.

BBC News (1998) The second fall of Veronica Guerin. *BBC News*, May 6. http://news.bbc.co.uk/2/hi/europe/86191.stm, accessed Jan. 11, 2008.

Becker, H. S. (1970) *Sociological Work: Method and Substance*. Chicago: Aldine.

Belsey, A., and Chadwick, R. (1992) *Ethical Issues in Journalism and the Media*. London: Routledge.

Blomfield, A. (2006) Is this the killer of Russian journalist? *Telegraph*, Oct. 10. http://www.telegraph.co.uk/news/main.jhtml?xml=/news/2006/10/09/wrussia09.xml, accessed Feb. 18, 2008.

Bollinger, L. (2003) President Bollinger's statement on the future of journalism education. *Columbia News*, Apr. 17. http://www.columbia.edu/cu/news/03/04/lcb_j_task_force.html, accessed Feb. 17, 2008.

Carey, J. (1980) The university tradition in journalism education. *Carleton Journalism Review*, 2(6), 3–7.

Dickinson, R. (2007) Accomplishing journalism: towards a revived sociology of a media occupation. *Cultural Sociology*, 1(2), 189–208.

Gilligan, C. (1982) *In a Different Voice: Psychological Theory and Women's Development*. Cambridge, MA: Harvard University Press.

Hayes, A., Singer, J., and Ceppos, J. (2007) Shifting roles, enduring values: the credible journalist in a digital age. *Journal of Mass Media Ethics*, 22(4), 262–279.

IPI (n.d.) Veronica Guerin. *International Press Institute's 50 World Press Freedom Heroes*. http://www.freemedia.at/Heroes_IPIReport2.00/20Guerin.htm, accessed Feb. 18, 2008.

Kohlberg, L. (1981) *The Philosophy of Moral Development: Moral Stages and the Idea of Justice*. San Francisco: Harper & Row.

Laville, S. (1999) Veronica Guerin Praise for reporter as second man gets life. *Telegraph*, July 30. http://www.telegraph.co.uk/htmlContent.jhtml?=/archive/1999/07/30/nveron30.html, accessed Jan. 11, 2008.

Masters, C. (1992) *Inside Story*. Sydney: Angus & Robertson.

Masters, C. (2001) Interview for the 40th year of Four Corners. http://www.abc.net.au/4corners/4c40/interviews/masters.htm, accessed Aug. 2, 2008.

Muir, H. (1996) Journalist who exposed underworld is shot dead. *Telegraph*, June 27. http://www.telegraph.co.uk/htmlContent.jhtml?=/archive/1996/06/27/whack27.html, accessed Jan. 11, 2008.

Observer (2006) Russian journalist shot dead. *Observer*, Oct. 7. http://www.guardian.co.uk/world/2006/oct/07/theobserver, accessed Jan. 11, 2008.

Parfitt, T. (2006) Assassin's bullet kills fiery critic of Putin. *Observer*, Oct. 8. http://www.guardian.co.uk/world/2006/oct/08/media.pressandpublishing, accessed Feb. 18, 2008.

Piaget, J. (1968) *The Moral Judgment of the Child* [circa 1932], trans. Marjorie Gabain. London: Routledge & Kegan Paul.

Randall, D. (2000) *The Universal Journalist*, 2nd edn. London: Pluto Press.

Sacks, J. (2001) In a world run by MTV, nobody has time to think. *Daily Telegraph*, Sept. 6.

Sanders, K. (2003) *Ethics and Journalism*. London: Sage.

Sydney Morning Herald (2008) Charges over death of journalist. *Sydney Morning Herald*, June 19.

Taylor, C. (2003) Veronica Guerin. *Salon*, Oct. 17. http://dir.salon.com/story/ent/movies/review/2003/10/17/veronica/, accessed Jan. 10, 2008.

Wershba, J. (n.d.) Edward R. Murrow and the time of his time. *Eve's Magazine*. http://www.evesmag.com/murrowx.htm, accessed Aug. 2, 2008.

Index

Index

226

CPSIA information can be obtained at www.ICGtesting.com
Printed in the USA
BVOW02*1455060214

343684BV00009B/86/P